Where

Is the

Body?

Discovering the Church in the Heart of Israel

Victor Schlatter

Treasure House

An Imprint of
Destiny Image® Publishers, Inc.
P.O. Box 310
Shippensburg, PA 17257-0310

ISBN 1-56043-339-6

For Worldwide Distribution
Printed in the U.S.A.

6 7 8 9 10 11 12 / 09 08 07 06 05

This book and all other Destiny Image, Revival Press, MercyPlace, Fresh Bread, Destiny Image Fiction, and Treasure House books are available at Christian bookstores and distributors worldwide.

For a U.S. bookstore nearest you, call **1-800-722-6774**.
For more information on foreign distributors, call **717-532-3040**.
Or reach us on the Internet: **www.destinyimage.com**

This is what the Lord Almighty says: "In those days ten men from all languages and nations will take firm hold of one Jew by the hem of his robe and say, 'Let us go with you, because we have heard that God is with you' " (Zechariah 8:23).

Dedication

Dedicated to Abraham's best Friend,
along with all of His family
from both sides of the Olive Tree.

Endorsements

"Author Victor Schlatter has accomplished a very commendable endeavor by writing on the subject of Israel, the Jewish people, and the Church in this book. He clearly makes his case that the Jew and the non-Jewish Christian is 'of one family growing together…of two olive trees grafted into one, waiting for their Lord to appear.' His insight into the meaning of the 'mystery' mentioned by St. Paul in his Letters to the Romans and to the Ephesians, clarifies the 'secret' of how the believing Jew and Gentile come to be part of the Kingdom of God. The Body has two parts or two identical halves—what an honor to be a part of one of those halves! Our appreciation to Mr. Schlatter for working through this theological and historical issue, especially as it relates to the modern Jewish State of Israel."

—George Giacumakis, Ph.D.
Professor of History
Director of the Mission Viejo Campus
California State University, Fullerton
Chairman of the Board, International Christian Embassy, Jerusalem

"This book will not be comfortable reading for many in the Christian Church; it challenges a whole number of widely held ideas that have no source in either the Old or New Testaments, but arise from Christianized

Hellenism. It therefore needs to be read thoughtfully and prayerfully. Victor Schlatter has done us all a very real service in writing it."

—Lance Lambert
Speaker, lecturer, teacher on Israel

"Where Is the Body? takes a fresh look at the Church's relationship to Israel and the Jewish people, which is a must in these days when Bible prophecy needs a proper anchor to keep it from flying off into the realm of fantasy. Today, many are reassessing this relationship in light of the reality of a regathered Israel, Christians rediscovering their 'Jewish roots' and Christian and Jewish scholars studying the Bible together—including the New Testament and the words of Jesus. Is this not what God intended from the beginning? I believe that Victor Schlatter has 'rightly divided' the Word of God to bring insight into Paul's words to the Ephesians concerning Jews and Gentiles, 'For He Himself [Jesus] is our peace, who has made the two one...to create in Himself one new man...thus making peace' (Eph. 2:14-15). This book is a must for every serious student of the Bible."

—Clarence H. Wagner, Jr.
International Director
Bridges for Peace
Jerusalem, Israel

"I sincerely believe that this book presents one of the most important truths found in the New Testament for all who want to experience the fullness of Christ's life. It is also one of the most neglected truths today, even though it was so near to the apostle Paul's heart. Rev. Schlatter's presentation and style are superb."

—Marvin Byers
Author, *The Final Victory: The Year 2000?*

"This is a fascinating and provocative book. Victor Schlatter exposes the anti-Semitism that so often distorts evangelical life and thought, and he makes a strong case for a theology that centers on God's deep and abiding love for Israel and Jewish people. I came away from reading his discussion with new insights into the unity of the Biblical message."

—Richard J. Mouw, Ph.D.
President, Fuller Theological Seminary
Pasadena, California, USA

"This is a timely book! The coming of a new millennium and the struggle to find a peace arrangement which will satisfy both Israelis and Arabs, to say nothing about the rest of the world, serve as a backdrop to consider Victor Schlatter's message of the Jew and Gentile family of God. Those who hold that the church has replaced Israel as God's chosen people will be confronted with the unifying message of the Old and New Testaments. This message needs to be addressed by the Christian community. After examining his arguments, I was moved to a greater understanding of what God has in store for His people."

—Robert E. Cooley, Chancellor
Gordon-Conwell Theological Seminary
South Hamilton, Massachusetts, USA

Contents

Foreword

Books on Israel abound, and any respectable Christian bookstore will, thus, carry a large selection of them. So, we may ask, what makes this book different? First, it is written by a man who has been in the field of service for many years, and his experience and maturity in the things of God and of Jesus his Lord are the foundation of this book. Second, the author has enjoyed a "hands-on" relationship with Israel and Jewish people for many years. This means that, third, he is well qualified to write a book of this nature. I believe this book will greatly edify you, the reader, because not only does it give good teaching, but it also reveals a lot of heart and warmth. For Victor Schlatter, the people of Israel are not theological entities or objects of prophetic interest only. No, they are real people who have suffered as no other people upon the earth have, and they are in need of our love, comfort, and care.

As you read this book, you will find your heart warmed, and you will be challenged by the author's insights and conclusions. This book will definitely help you to understand with greater clarity the purposes of God for Israel, and it will enable you to appreciate your role in this great end-time adventure. Most of all, it will blow away some of the accepted, but not biblically verified, thinking that has taken hold of the Church through the centuries with regard to Israel and the Jewish people.

Much of this thinking goes back to the Constantinian period of the fourth century, and it has been a cause of great pain and heartache to the Jewish people. So, I encourage you to read Victor Schlatter's book, and read it carefully, for in it you will discern the voice of God and you will thereby be better equipped to love and serve Him.

It is then with great joy that I commend this book and its author to you.

Rev. Malcolm Hedding
Chairman, Christian Action for Israel
Natal, South Africa
November 1998

Introduction

Few people who take the Bible seriously—and quite a few who don't—would vigorously dispute the fact that the world is surging headlong into apocalyptic times, or more simply put, "the last days."

But how last is *last*? Readily dismissing the pseudo prophets who give us dates and charts that the sober mind has little disposition to embrace, our subconscious dutifully assures us that the "end" will hardly fall within this month's budget of time. One must even wonder if the date and event programmers themselves are even all that convinced of their own predictions.

Not to worry—in the longer tenure of events, we all do pretty well, knowing that sooner or later this insane globe is headed for one more "Big Bang." But this time around we perceive that this must result in something of a social and political convulsion of most unsavory proportions. It can't be otherwise, but our mental comfort zone often prompts us to project this event to a time that is a bit later down the track. After all, there's just no way that we could fit it in until after the holidays!

So with that on the back burner, it may be appropriate to scan the horizon and the Word of God for a few fresh ideas on what helpful signposts we might be looking for. This is a far more significant system of watching, if indeed not a more scriptural one, than generating all kinds of charts and deadlines.

I say, "fresh ideas" because these pages will not reflect the time-worn predictions that are promoted by much of the evangelical teachings, clichés, and assumptions that are constantly declining in credibility as we move into the ever-increasing materialism-come-frustration of a post-civilization, post-Christian mentality.

With tongue in cheek, I boast of having earned my advanced degree at the same University that Moses did. He got his secular education at Pharaoh Tech in Egypt, and then he earned his Doctorate at M.I.T., that is, the "Midian Institute of Theology" on the backside of the Arabian desert.

I traveled much the same educational route. My original degree was in science from a reasonably renowned Mid-Western university in the USA, which was followed by bits and pieces of diversified exposure to various graduate studies. But my most cherished degree came from quite another M.I.T., not unlike the one where Moses attained his greatest intellectual strides. In a region tucked far away in the backblocks of the Southern Highlands of Papua New Guinea, we translated the Scriptures for a tribal people who, at our arrival, were just peeking out of the Stone Age. It was in these rugged and isolated mountain villages that the Eternal Teacher pointed out realities from the Book that I was handling that I had hitherto never seen—and perhaps never could have seen—in my original Western setting.

So it is with the insights that have formulated and gelled through the course of some three decades of unconventional academic exposure that I unfold to you the following chapters. In fact, the first root awakenings for this book began to germinate in the mid-1970's as I translated chapter 11 of the New Testament Book of Revelation into the vernacular of the some 40,000 strong Waola nation. I began to see things about the end of days that the theological teachers who spoke to my earlier years had never, ever bothered to tell me. As the many blanks began to be filled in, the truth ultimately emerged.

So without further ado, let us proceed together to allow some of these early seeds to sprout and grow as we jointly probe the question: Really now, *Where **Is** the Body?*

> *The disciples spoke up and asked, "Where, Lord?" He said, "Where the body is, there too will the vultures gather"* (Luke 17:37 NJB).

Victor Schlatter
Jerusalem
October 1998

Chapter 1

A Man Called Abraham

The Bible is not a recipe book designed to detail the proper blend of responses to a god that is hungry[1] for some sort of gourmet lifestyle. Nor is the Bible a rulebook, as multitudes would presume it to be, to instruct us just "how to get there." This mentality puts an unrealistic focus either on human abilities or on the whims of the deity—or both. This is hardly the God we find revealed in Scripture. Rather the record of Scripture is primarily a presentation of God's relationship with man, where divine wisdom, or a blend of it, is demonstrated to be of far greater significance than a set of rigid rules.

In no way does this insight set aside the Ten Commandments and their related precepts as incidental. These principles are monumental. They are certainly not "Ten Suggestions" as some of our currently enlightened theologians might unwittingly imply to a "free and liberated" society. But they could potentially become dusty texts and the unfortunate roots of legalism without the proper epoxy of the Divine Presence—the Holy Spirit who cements us into a conscious trust relationship with a Father God.

---

1.   Ps. 50:12.

Where Is the Body?

Thus the real bridging of the chasm dividing mortal mankind from the eternal—the closing of that gulf between the created and his Creator—starts with the account of a man called Abraham, which can be found 12 chapters into the Scriptures.

Abraham's predecessors, Adam, Noah, Enoch, *et al*, certainly give us some genuine clues of proper and improper responses to our Maker. But the really basic insights start to be revealed in Genesis 12. The bond of friendship of Abraham with his God is rooted in trust and obedience, which is a world away from legalism. What a pity that so many multitudes of the self-proclaimed "faithful" have missed that most essential cue to intimacy with their own God.

In Genesis 12, the Almighty calls Abraham into His "office"[2] and says, "Look, My friend, I've got a job for you." Abraham promptly responds in the affirmative, and the restoration of an impaired relationship between a God and His creation takes a giant stride forward.

Let's look at how it happened:

The Lord had said to Abram, "Leave your country, your people and your father's household and go to the land I will show you. I will make you into a great nation and I will bless you; I will make your name great, and you will be a blessing. I will bless those who bless you, and whoever curses you I will curse; and all peoples on earth will be blessed through you" (Genesis 12:1-3).

In simple summary, God tells Abraham—the new name God had given him in the course of his new assignment[3]—to remove himself from his present surroundings and go to a land that He would show him for the express purpose of creating His family, indeed a family of nations.

Of special note, which is definitely not to be overlooked throughout the ensuing chapters, is the divine umbrella of blessing and cursing that

---

2. My first thought was that this expression may be a mite too casual, but on reflection, I concluded—*Where else is His office but the human heart?*

3. *Abram* means "honored father," but *Abraham* means "father of many nations" (see Gen. 17:1-8).

2

the Almighty positioned over that family. God's purpose in this heavenly oriented covering was, interestingly enough, not based on performance[4] but on His underlying intent to preserve this family for His ultimate redemptive purposes. Anyone who touched God's "kids" would suffer the consequences. Anyone who helped them along the way, would be rewarded in kind. The option to evaluate the family's performance was never left to the kings, presidents, popes, pastors, or even individuals from among the nations. Tyrants and dictators from Pharaoh to Nebuchadnezzar, from Haman to Hitler, and now from Yasser Arafat to Hamas and Hizbullah have missed the message and gotten burned, but ironically, the nations have never learned their lesson. God has His own agenda for His family. Don't mess with it!

As for Abraham, his original haunts were, of course, near Babylon, which is right next door to modern Baghdad, not a terribly popular place with most of Abraham's offspring today. Moreover, Babylon also has an even more negative stigma for Bible believers of the last days, so it wasn't a bad idea for Abraham to clear out of there when he did.

And speaking of haunts, that choice of terminology has its significance because it was hardly due to poor soil that the Almighty had Abraham pull up roots. The demonic realm that held sway over the entire area[5] was not exactly the sort of environment that impressed El Shaddai. So He proposed a deal with His new friend that He and He alone was to be his God from then on. Indeed, this would have been the most basic by-law of their unwritten contract, for the Almighty had not the slightest tolerance for sharing power or glory with any other pseudo-deities. Now some

---

4.   Quite apart from God's pronouncement of blessing or cursing on the attitude of the nations toward His people Israel, God also gave a parallel pronouncement of blessing or cursing to His own people, which was based on their performance. See Deuteronomy 28.

5.   *Abram*, as he was known before God changed his name to *Abraham*, was actually in temporary residence at Haran some 1,000 km. northwest of his birthplace, Ur, when the Lord challenged him to make another move on to Caanan. Nevertheless, the same demonic forces that ruled the minds and lives of the pagan population of his native Ur were spread throughout the whole of the region and were rife at Haran as well.

4,000 years down the track of history, this premise still is, in fact, bedrock for all no-nonsense sons of Abraham today: "Hear, O Israel! The LORD is our God, the LORD alone."[6]

Abraham quite readily agreed with God's proposal, and the stage was now set for a new era of a trust relationship between man to his maker. For himself and for his extended family for all ages to come, the soul of Abraham clutched to what his eyes could not yet see.

The land that Abraham and his entourage set out for was called Canaan according to the text[7], and the Canaanites, the offspring of Ham[8] happened to inhabit the land at that time. The record indicates, however, that God had a parallel operation to effect. The Canaanites had become so morally corrupt that He simultaneously designed to remove them once and for all in a stroke of judgment to purge the land of its decadence and perversion.[9]

But how does a single family—albeit an extended family unit— conquer an entire land filled with wild-eyed pagan warriors, cruel kings, and a dearth of moral scruples? Survival, even to the more hardy of clans, might pose a problem.

It is noted in Chapter 14 of Genesis that Abraham's entourage did include a reasonably healthy security staff, numbering in excess of 300, and that he did get into an altercation or two with some of the local power players in the land. Surprisingly, he came out the better. But even with these preliminary successes—however large or limited they may have been—a new clan of alien visitors from up north would have been peanuts compared to the tribal structures already in place. How did he gain acceptance for even an opening bid on one small corner?

---

6. Deut. 6:4 from *The TANAKH: The New JPS Translation According to the Traditional Hebrew Text.* Copyright 1985 by the Jewish Publication Society. Used by permission.

7. Gen. 12:5.

8. Gen. 10:6.

9. Gen. 15:16; 19:13; Lev. 18:28.

A Man Called Abraham

Abraham's triumph in the land was unique. He traveled the length and breadth of the land building altars to dedicate the land to the honor of the one and only living God. The first altar he built was at Shechem, the next one was near Bethel, then Hebron, and finally the most renowned of all on Mount Moriah, which ultimately turned out none other than the select spot where Solomon built his glorious temple.[10] That divine strategy was decisive. Abraham's emerging family had to come and go a few times over the centuries, but the Almighty to whom Abraham consecrated the land stayed on. This is a most fascinating linkage since it is underlined in God's reassurance to King Solomon after the dedication of his elaborate temple to the living God:

I have chosen and consecrated this temple so that My Name may be there forever. My eyes and My heart will always be there (2 Chronicles 7:16).

To this day there is a sense of awe in the proximity of the Western Wall, the last remaining vestige of Israel's now long-destroyed and desecrated second temple. The massive stones from Solomon's original structure were again used for the retaining wall of the second structure. Now this too is in ruins, but the celebrated Wall has long since become a hallowed place of prayer for the faithful. It is safe to say that millions of Jews—some observant, some not—along with a multitude of Bible-oriented Christians still sense the impact of the promise that "My Name [will] be there forever. My eyes and My heart will always be there."

Indeed, Canaan was the earlier name for the entire area. But God had a new designation to present, which is of such significance for the purposes of this book that I am obliged to emphasize it now and repeat it throughout our discussion. God's initial expression to identify the land was not *Israel* and certainly not *Palestine*. Rather it is referred to at least 20 times in Deuteronomy as, "The place He [chose] as a dwelling for His Name."[11] This is of utmost consequence for any and all Bible believers

---

10. Gen. 12:7-8; 13:18; 22:2,9.

11. Deut. 14:23.

today who would make sense of the whirlwinds of controversy that sweep this land in its current political confusion, violent confrontations, and multiplicity of claims that are basically without human resolution.

Israel, of course, was the recognized name of the land of the children of Israel, who under Joshua conquered and drove out the Canaanites at the irreversible decree of the God of Abraham. As such, the land was thus renamed after the declaration of statehood of the reborn Israel on May 14, 1948.

But the name *Palestine* is the misnomer of the ages. When Roman Emperor Hadrian leveled Jerusalem in A.D. 132 (a second devastation 62 years after Titus razed the city and destroyed the temple), he was so bitterly incensed with the Jews that he vowed that there would no longer be a Judea to retain any memory of them either historically or linguistically. Rather, he declared that it would forever after be known as *Falastina*—chiding the Jews with the mental specter of their (and God's) age-old enemies the Philistines. Emperor Hadrian rubbed all the salt he could into their bitter wounds of tragic defeat in battle, loss of their land, and one more devastation of their beloved Jerusalem.

The name *Falastina*, or *Palestine*, stuck to that degree that subsequent kings of the earth relished it, to the point that even maps in printed Bibles accepted it. The United Nations today also savors the name, recognizing a people labeled by a most inapplicable designation: "Palestinians."

One of the great political injustices seeping out of the contaminated cisterns of anti-Semitic Rome was renaming the land of our Lord in honor of Goliath and his cruel cohorts. Unfortunately that contamination has these days even oozed into streams that supposedly represent the waters of life. The misfortune that parts of the Church have bought into this "sleight of hand" is nothing short of appalling. No, Goliath and his people are hardly alive and well today, but their mentor the devil is; and he plays the substitution card of the long-departed Philistines to the maximum and continues to deceive the multitudes some three millennia after their passing.

A Man Called Abraham

Former Prime Minister of Israel, Golda Meir, frequently declared "There is no Palestinian nation."[12] That more than accurate assessment was also supported by no less an arch enemy of the Jewish people than Syrian president Hafez al Assad who has been recorded as declaring: "There is no such thing as a Palestinian people, there is no Palestinian entity, there is only Syria."[13] We might find very little else palatable in this cruel dictator's pronouncements, but in this case he opened his mouth to reinforce the truth. The so-called Palestinians are—like the Syrians— Arabs, primarily sons of Ishmael who had followed their Jewish cousins back to a once-desolate land in the late 1800's. Some were in pursuit of economic opportunities, as evidence of land revitalization became apparent. Unfortunately, others followed with a grim determination to never let their Jewish kinfolk get a foothold in the land again. They failed.

But to this day terrorist Arafat (alias Chairman Arafat, or an even greater mockery "President" Arafat) and his murderous mob have not given up in their efforts, whether by war or a pseudo "peace," to drive the Jews into oblivion. Twenty-eight out of 33 clauses of the Palestinian Covenant drafted in 1964 call for the complete destruction and annihilation of Israel. At the time of this writing, five full years after the signing of the 1993 Oslo Peace Accords, worthless promises made to amend the Covenant have proven nothing more than empty deception.[14] To add insult to injury, Arafat's own official organization, *Fatah*, has continued unabated to trumpet the same violent threats over the Internet.[15]

But Canaan-come-Israel, then "Palestine," and now back to Israel, sounds like so much political rhetoric which is still searching for a political answer. Much better that we opt for the biblically inspired place

---

12. Nissam Mishal, *Those Were the Years* (Tel Aviv: Miskal Publishing Distribution, Ltd., 1998), 153.

13. Jamblatt, *I Speak for Lebanon* (London: Zed, 1982), 78. Cited by Benjamin Netanyahu in *A Place Among the Nations* (New York: Bantam, 1993), 96.

14. Quoted in "An Oslo Scorecard," *Middle East Intelligence Digest*, September 1998, 3.

15. Accessible on website http://www.fateh.org. Copies are also available from the author.

where "the Lord has chosen to put His name" and let the rightful ownership flow from there. It is a place where much violent history has transpired and where it is all happening once more today. Her capital, which is known as the City of Peace, has ironically seen less peace and more bloodshed than most cites of countless other nations and evil empires from antiquity to the present. But if we know the Scriptures, the days of Jerusalem's prophetic destiny are at last soon to come.

And, of course, this is the very land where the Almighty told Abraham to go build His family. Build a family he did. This is exactly where God's redemptive plans for that family of Israel—not to mention an extension to all the nations—begin.

Chapter 2

The Law: Thou Shalt Not Get It Confused

Some six centuries down the line from Abraham, God groomed and commissioned another man named Moses. Moses is most commonly known for leading the family that Abraham had fathered out of slavery in Egypt. But with the Jews he has even a higher niche in history. He met with God on the top of Mount Sinai and received from the Almighty a code of living that outlined how His family might best conduct themselves as a people to be set apart. God gave His people His *Torah* Law through Moses.

And this brings us to a very key insight. It is almost too simple to be missed, but overlooked it has been! The Jew does not *"keep the Law"* to *become a Jew*. He keeps the Law *because he is a Jew*. Even as a child I absorbed from my environment the very uninformed, if not anti-Semitic, stereotype that "the Jew thinks he's saved because he keeps the Law." Well, he doesn't. In fact, the Old Testament concept of salvation is quite apart from what the Church understands today.

The Jew does not think in terms of individual salvation. He looks for the redemption of Israel, the salvation of the nation. He is aware of God's indelible promises to Abraham, and it is in these promises that he anchors his hope. Paul the apostle quite sufficiently summarizes it:

And so all Israel will be saved, as it is written: "The deliverer will come from Zion; He will turn godlessness away from Jacob. And this is My covenant with them when I take away their sins" (Romans 11:26-27).

The observant Jew, therefore, wants to be a part of that redemption. Obviously he desires to maintain a level of identity and compliance worthy to be counted in the nation. But beyond that, there's nothing individualistic about it. It's a family affair with a God to heed and standards to maintain.

This is not a bad lesson for certain pseudo-Christian mentalities. I have long chafed at the self-centered presumption of the "professional" sinner who has corrupted his own life and countless around him only to finally, on his own timetable, get things fixed up with the Judge in a *personal effort to save himself* from damnation. Without a doubt, his ambition to ultimately do the right thing is par excellence. But why has he done it? If the drive that propels him is merely to outmaneuver God and save his own skin, his motivation is something far less than virtuous. Is it not much more noble to join forces with the Almighty *because He alone is right* than to fall in line just to get off the hook? But even for the naïve who plod along so far behind at a sometimes unbelievable distance, I find His grace continues to be immense.

And so it was through that grace that God eventually presented His Messiah. It was in an era when Greek cosmology had effected a more specific concept of the afterlife, including a Heaven and hell. This has had a profound influence on the Christian view of individualistic salvation, giving rise as well to the potential of a far more personal identity with one's God than the ordinary Jew would ever envision—except, that is, for those in the camp of the likes of Abraham, Moses, and King David.

On the other hand, Moses gave "the family" the keys to a good life, and the observant Jew thus keeps the Law to live a lifestyle set apart for his God. As the tenth chapter of Romans clearly bears out, there most certainly is a "…righteousness that is by the law,"[1] but it is restricted to the here and now as careful study of the entire passage along with related texts will confirm.

In Chapter 6, we will deal in greater depth with a spiritually debilitating virus inflicting many Christians that we might call "paganization" and which will follow in a direct relationship with the insights we have made above. However at this point, we must yet shatter one more less than helpful myth about the Mosaic Law—that is, that the Law is primarily about diet. It's not. Diet is often brought into the spotlight because it's the simplest baton to wave. However, if one analyzes the Book of Deuteronomy verse by verse, you will find that only about two percent pertains to diet. Jesus also made it crystal clear that a summary of the whole Law was about relationships—a relationship to Almighty God and relationships with one another.[2] It is noteworthy that reputable rabbis, ancient and modern, taught and still teach quite the same principle.

All this divinely determined purpose of the Law comes straight out of the Bible for all who choose to see it. After he declares the sacred decrees of the Almighty to His children on a vast number of issues, Moses in the Book of Deuteronomy again underlines the designated end:

The Lord commanded us to obey all these decrees and to fear the Lord our God, so that we might always prosper and be kept alive, as is the case today. And if we are careful to obey all this law before the Lord our God, as He has commanded us, that will be our righteousness (Deuteronomy 6:24-25).

In summary, Moses was saying that if you do what God has told you:

1. You will prosper.

2. Your life will be preserved.

3. This will be your *righteousness*.

---

1. Rom. 10:5a.

2. Mt. 22:37-40.

In other words, in your obedience you will have a good living. You will have a *long* life. Your life will have God's stamp of favor—a relationship with the Almighty.

There is no mention of Heaven, hell, or salvation at this point! The Jew keeps the Law not *to be* family, but because he *is* family.

Although I in no way want to disparage the value of observing the principles of God's *Torah* for Jew or Gentile for any or all reasons expressed throughout this discussion, those unfortunates who miss the mark most widely are the Gentile cults who have developed a tendency to measure their divine status by their capacity to keep the Law. For sure, this attitude would cause the Grand Umpire to call, "Strike one!" May we all hope that it will not deteriorate to strike three!

One of the most meaningful reflections on a Gentile believer's dietary restrictions[3] was expressed to me a few years ago by a very dear Jewish brother—a Messianic follower of Yeshua. He stated emphatically that he can find nowhere in Scripture anything indicating that a Gentile cannot go to Heaven if he eats pork. In fact, he mused, "He might even get there a bit quicker!"

Moses elaborates more in the following chapter of Deuteronomy:

But it was because the Lord loved you and kept the oath He swore to your forefathers that He brought you out with a mighty hand and redeemed you from the land of slavery, from the power of Pharaoh king of Egypt. Know therefore that the Lord your God is God; He is the faithful God, keeping His covenant of love to a thousand generations of those who love Him and keep His commands (Deuteronomy 7:8-9).

His initial redemption was from the slavery in Egypt, and His love relationship was to a thousand generations in the here and now. One Jewish concept of eternal life is to live on in your children and your children's children. Moses continues to further describe God's love for His family:

3.　For a complete discussion on a guide to Gentile dietary observance from the New Testament, see Acts 15:1-31.

The Law: Thou Shalt Not Get It Confused

Therefore, take care to follow the commands, decrees and laws I give you today. If you pay attention to these laws and are careful to follow them, then the Lord your God will keep His covenant of love with you, as He swore to your forefathers. He will love you and bless you and increase your numbers. He will bless the fruit of your womb, the crops of your land—your grain, new wine and oil—the calves of your herds and the lambs of your flocks in the land that He swore to your fore-fathers to give you. You will be blessed more than any other people; none of your men or women will be childless, nor any of your livestock without young. The Lord will keep you free from every disease (Deuteronomy 7:11-15a).

Again this sounds pretty much like a hoped for heaven on earth. The Jew's relationship with his God is repeatedly described as being in the here and now. So it is not surprising that in the New Testament the apostle Paul flows in the same stream:

Moses describes in this way the righteousness that is by the law: "The man who does these things will live by them" (Romans 10:5).

God's righteous reward from the Law is a good life—a life of blessing. The *Torah* is full of this kind of promise: If you do the right things, you'll live a good life and a long life.

But then Paul goes on to make his point that there has now been uncovered a hitherto unnoticed promise of faithfulness from a righteous God, in that, by a trust in His Messiah, His people will not only have the blessing of their Father for the here and now, but they will be able to receive it forever as they participate in an intimate family relationship with their God.

I have read Romans for years—or should I say *misread*—presuming that Paul is saying that the Law of God as expressed through Moses is now a bit of deadwood to be discarded. He never says this at all!

Is God's precious *Torah*—the Word He ultimately chose to make flesh—deadwood? I'm afraid this hand-me-down teaching comes from

13

reading Paul with "anti-Semitic tinted glasses" and borders on blasphemy. These were the only Scriptures that Jesus ever held. He loved them, lived them, and quoted from them.

I suggest the serious student study those texts from Romans again—all of them. Paul is saying that the righteousness of the Law is a temporal beginning for the here and now, but that a relationship sealed in the heavenlies with God's *Ruach Ha Kodesh*—the Hebrew expression for the holy breath of God—will add a *forever* dimension to the family both individually and collectively. Transitory or not, that beginning Mosaic stepping stone to the Almighty was ordered and ordained by the Designer of time and space and is hardly to be scoffed at by Jew or Gentile. And so it was that Moses was God's faithful channel at God's appointed time and hardly left a legality that was eventually to be plowed under.

*   *   *

"Abraham, you go to the land where I have chosen to put My name and raise up My family."

"Moses, you're next. You teach My family what a good life is all about."

And then we have One more....

Chapter 3

Kinship Signed in Blood

The third player on the stage turned out to take the lead role in the drama. Paul declares in the New Testament Book of Galatians:

But when the time had fully come, God sent forth His Son... (Galatians 4:4 RSV).

Although He at times functioned as a prophet, this was certainly not His role. A great teacher He also was, and obviously eloquent beyond any comparable precedent. But neither was He primarily sent as a great teacher. In fact, other than His implication on some occasions and unmistakable demonstration on others that God was most certainly His Father-Source, He taught nothing new that other good rabbis before Him—and even others after—did not teach as well.

Nor was He a "second God"—a sort of deity in reserve—parachuted miraculously from the heavenlies to somehow complement the Number One. This concept is from pagan influence upon the Church from the Dark Ages and before[1] and is hardly presented from His own lips or from anywhere else in Scripture. If anything is bedrock to the Jew—as well as

---

1. In fact, we would hardly be surprised that this pagan concept had a hand in fomenting the Dark Ages!

15

our own Christian roots in Abraham—it is the fact that Father Abraham turned a corner to serve one and one only God. Thus it is this reflection by certain less than careful Christian theologians, who unwittingly tend to undo the enlightened monotheistic course of Abraham, that gives such pain to our Jewish brethren.

This brings to mind my unique encounter with an observant Jew some years ago near the Western Wall, which is sometimes less tactfully referred to as the Wailing Wall. It occurred during the biblical *Sukkot* holidays. I and my band of Papua New Guinean pilgrims were milling on the Western Wall plaza near the sacred *Kotel*—the most distinct remnant of the massive retaining wall of the second temple where the faithful come to pray. My companions had come up from the South Pacific all the way to Jerusalem for the biblical *Sukkot*, known in English as the Feast of Tabernacles. With their brightly coloured knit caps and vivacious smiles, Papua New Guinean believers are hardly low-profile anywhere.

It was then that we ran into this Israeli man probably in his thirties. He wore a small *kippa* on his head, indicating that he was an observant Jew, that is, that he recognized, prayed to, and served the same Creator God that we did. He most certainly had come down to the Wall for the very purpose of prayer. Obviously our Papua New Guinean contingent had attracted his fancy. He asked where we originated from.

"We're Christians from Papua New Guinea, but we're probably not the kind of Christians that you would be too familiar with. We have a deep love and respect for Israel, and we have come up to the Feast in Jerusalem to bless and support you. We recognize the land of Israel as your God-given heritage and we want to encourage you to never give it away. We appreciate your God and your Bible...." And then quite unprogrammed, for some reason (that Reason that usually becomes amazingly manifest after the fact), I abruptly postulated, "You Jews think we Christians have three Gods, don't you?"

Almost automatically, he nodded in the affirmative.

Kinship Signed in Blood

I continued, "Who is God anyway? He's so vast, so indefinable He's beyond the description of any human words; He's so holy that you would be reluctant to even utter His name." He wholeheartedly agreed.

And I went on, "And who is the *Ruach Ha Kodesh?*" That's the Hebrew for the "Holy Wind" or Holy Spirit.

Answering my own question, I pressed my point, "That is God's means, His designated manner of connection between us and His Presence as a holy, inexpressible, indescribable, and unapproachable God. Is that two Gods?" I queried.

"No," he enjoined reflexively.

"So, who is Jesus?" I continued, "I certainly believe that He had a special supernatural birth, but He was born with a human body just like ours. You cut Him, and He bled. He knew pain."

He was following me intently. Any further pros or cons of my concept of the miraculous were quite irrelevant and would have been totally counterproductive.

I continued, "But I believe that Jesus"—perhaps I said *"Yeshua"*— "was so filled with the *Ruach Ha Kodesh* that He was God's special presentation to us."

My newfound orthodox friend added instinctively, "I can buy that!"

And in the treasuries of the Kingdom, perhaps his new "purchase" was at that point already being processed. If not then, I perceived that it soon would be.

I'll value that encounter forever. What evil, what pain, what isolation is created by using words of confrontation, arrogance, bigotry, and even preconceived judgment! The hour has come to embrace our brothers and sisters in love, that they will appropriate and enjoy the entirety of what their Father has pre-programmed for them.

Where Is the Body?

And he could "buy it," not only because it falls within a valid definition of the one and only true God, but because that description falls within the parameters spelled out by Scripture itself.

In a confrontation with the Pharisees within this very whirlpool of semantics, Jesus quoted Psalm 82 where the Almighty addresses His subordinate creation as "gods."[2] Jesus makes the point that if even God sets the precedent by referring to human beings as "gods," what could be the big problem in His referring to Himself as "God's son"? The human biological linkage was in obvious evidence through Mary's divine obedience and participation—believe what they would about her chastity. Yet the corresponding spiritual linkage with the God of Heaven that set Jesus beyond the pale of mere humanity, was that He was so filled with His Father's *Ruach Ha Kodesh* that He bore that preeminent claim of sonship. His very life and authority testified to all who would accurately observe who His real Father was.

But the beauty of it all is that from the dawn of the universe—and that takes us back a year or two—it was the eternal intention of the God of Abraham that His family should ultimately be like Him. Shaped by the model of His firstborn and filled with His Spirit, the plan was—and still is for that matter—that we are programmed to be "like Jesus." But are we?

At those precise times when we are anointed and filled with the Father's power, we are to be exactly what He intended us to be, to function exactly as He intended us to function and to obey exactly as He intended for us to obey. Obviously there are many lapses—too many lapses. The difference with God's firstborn Son was that there were no lapses.

It was Paul the apostle who referred to Him as, "firstborn among many brothers"[3] and the "...firstfruits of those who have fallen asleep."[4]

---

2. Ps. 82:6; Jn. 10:34. Most English versions take this to mean that God is directing His discourse to actual errant human beings, and Jesus seems to apply it in this direction.

3. Rom. 8:29.

4. 1 Cor. 15:20; see also verse 23.

Kinship Signed in Blood

In addition, the author of the Book of Hebrews, in his second chapter, leaves little doubt of how God presented His Son as the ultimate expression of what He desired the rest of us to be: Spirit-filled sons and daughters of the Most High.

But over and above His emergence as the firstborn of the Father in an expression of divinely designed God-infused holiness for His family was Yeshua's presentation of His absolute obedience as a blood atonement for sin for all humankind. The Spirit of God Himself so filled a preordained body of clay that He became the Lamb of atonement "without blemish or defect,"[5] "the Lamb of God who takes away the sin of the world."[6]

The story of Abraham's intended sacrifice of his son Isaac is a fascinating preview to what actually did happen on that very same Mount Moriah some two millennia later.[7]

God, of course, intervened to reroute the whole procedure before any of Isaac's blood was shed, assuring Abraham that He now knew that Abraham would withhold nothing from his God. What the Genesis account does not spell out is the fact in retrospect that God was indirectly saying, "Abraham, this is not yet the time, nor are you the one to do it. I Myself will carry out the blood offering, in My own time and in My own way. It will be My Son."

Why God chose the interim sacrificial blood-letting of domestic animals in the first place is not mine to speculate here. It was, of course, a symbolic substitution to effect forgiveness for the one who sinned, a malady to be sure, of the entire race. And it is a principle without question

---

5.   1 Pet. 1:19.

6.   Jn. 1:29.

7.   Mount Moriah was the same site specified nearly 1,000 years later for the building of Solomon's temple. It is today the contested Temple Mount area dominated by the Muslim Dome of the Rock. The northernmost point of Moriah, however, which is well north of the mosque area, is the presumed site of Calvary. From numerous considerations, it is the most logical location of the actual crucifixion of Jesus. See Genesis 22 and Second Chronicles 3:1.

throughout Scripture that "The soul who sins is the one who will die."[8] Substituting the blood of an innocent animal was God's preferred way. I for one cannot and will not question it any more than I can question the slaughtering of animals for human diet.[9] I did hear a credible Rabbi, who favored the reinstitution of animal sacrifice for his people, saying recently that if one observed the sacrificial slaughter of an animal for his personal sin, he would depart from that ceremony a much more sober individual with respect to the gravity of his misdeeds. He does have a point!

But from my own Christian experience, the reality of that which I do see—coupled with my faith in what I do not see—I perceive that the ultimate was when God designed to occupy an especially prepared human form Himself with His very own *Ruach Ha Kodesh.*[10] And in that body, He would permit whatever venom and violence that might be done to Him by a depraved humanity that never tires in trying to play God in its resistance to a Sovereign Authority. And even though His own creation would endeavor to destroy Him, His final response was to reach back in love with a "Father, forgive them for they do not know what they are doing."[11] This was God's personal response to substitute Himself as a Lamb in human form for the atonement of mankind.

Ironic to some, perhaps quite plausible to others, 40 years after the supreme atonement of the Almighty, the magnificent temple of the God of Israel was for a second time in history razed to the ground and consumed with unholy fire. Now for almost 2,000 years the observant Jew, denied of his temple with its singular altar for sacrificial atonement, has had to make do without the designated access to his God. Rabbinic Judaism has improvised as best it could to stretch out its often-beleaguered hands to its Creator. Nevertheless a portion of Abraham's family had

---

8.　Ezek. 18:4b. See also such basic related texts as Genesis 2:17; 3:2 and Romans 3:23; 6:23.

9.　There are those who do question the practice, but sidetracking to that issue would be quite irrelevant to our purposes here.

10.　Heb. 10:5-7.

11.　Lk. 23:34.

found an answer of their own—"the Lamb of God, who takes away the sin of the world!"[12]

In these days of violence, confrontation, and kaleidoscopic tensions in Israel, many look for the eventual construction of a third temple. Most of these are overseas Christians who have a starry-eyed prophetic view of things to come with a very limited understanding of the political potential of such an innovation at this point of history. Although there is a small percentage of orthodox Jews who would certainly like to see it happen, Israel at large would regard it as most unrealistic.

It is the opinion of this author that there is no credible Scripture whatever that would suggest that a third temple must be rebuilt *before* the advent of Messiah. In fact, the *Haredim*, the most rigidly orthodox group within Judaism, just might have a handle on the issue in their insistence that no one should attempt to rebuild the temple. For they teach that the Messiah will bring the temple with Him when He comes. Interesting! We'll pick up on that idea again a few chapters down the line.

*   *   *

"Abraham, build Me a family. Moses teach them how to live. But I, Myself, will enter a third and final body filling it with My own *Ruach Ha Kodesh* to die as an atonement, a *kaparah*, for My own children who like everyone else will have quite missed the mark somewhere along the way—a family now fathered, taught, and provided for with redemption at last by a Father God who deeply cares."

---

12.   Jn. 1:29b.

Chapter 4

A Fractured Family

Then enter the family breakup that never should have happened. But it did. Of course, that's the sad story of all the channels and chasms cut by our sins and misdeeds in all the watercourses of life. They should never have happened—but they did.

So what *did* happen? The family split up. You can pick your friends, but you can't pick your relatives. And this was a particularly nasty family breakup.

It just so happened that half the family thought that Jesus was the greatest thing since the first sunrise.[1] But the other half were just plain jealous, and as we might suspect, this lot was comprised of much of the religious hierarchy of the day. Of course, we'd hardly find anything like this happening in Church politics these days, would we!

But the boys[2] in charge just didn't like Him. They didn't like His credentials[3]; they accused Him of blaspheming God; they misquoted Him. They twisted everything He said and basically misinterpreted much

---

1. Jn. 7:45-46.

2. This is somewhat of a twist, but not unlike Isaiah 3:4.

3. Mt. 27:18; see also Mt. 13:53-57.

23

of His teaching. Many ordinary people liked Him, and that made it all the worse. Jealousy can do a lot of unbelievable things—especially in a predominately religious setting. We know the well-worn statement that "power corrupts, and absolute power corrupts absolutely." With God in your hip pocket, who needs moral accuracy?

It didn't all happen right away, but eventually those who couldn't abide Him crystallized into one camp, and those who believed in Him gelled into another.

To those who believed who He was, He gave His parting commission:

...go and make disciples of all nations [the Gentiles—*goyim*] *baptizing them in the name of the Father and of the Son and of the Holy Spirit, and teaching them to obey everything I have commanded you* (Matthew 28:19-20a).

Luke also uses the term *nations* in his Gospel,[4] while in Acts he uses "ends of the earth,"[5] as does Mark in his record after first specifying going "into all the world."[6]

The choice of terms is significant. Although I doubt that anyone could or even would argue that the commission to go out is to be *totally exclusive* of Jewish ears, simple honest scrutiny of this and many related texts will indicate that the target audience implied is *primarily the non-Jewish Gentiles* who are to be *added* to the family. This is borne out as well in many of Paul's comments to the Ephesians and Romans, as we will see in later chapters, but it is likewise a fulfillment of God's initial promises to Abraham:

...and all peoples on earth will be blessed through you (Genesis 12:3).

Moreover, Jesus Himself gave at least three very clear indications of this culmination—certainly not a midpoint revision—of God's ultimate plan for all His creation. In the parable of the good Shepherd, He states:

---

4.   Lk. 24:47.

5.   Acts 1:8.

6.   Mk. 16:15.

24

A Fractured Family

I have other sheep that are not of this sheep pen. I must bring them also. They too will listen to my voice, and there shall be one flock and one shepherd (John 10:16).

When talking to the Samaritan woman sitting at Jacob's well, He declares:

...we worship what we do know for salvation is from the Jews (John 4:22b).

This was no more a racist comment than God's original promise to Abraham in using him to bless the world. Rather, it was one and the same, a factual representation of the Creator God's eternal plan to use the Jewish nation to prosper all humanity.

An even more specifically radical comment by Jesus, and one often swept under the carpet by suggesting it as a "test" of the woman's integrity, was Yeshua's encounter with the Canaanite woman near the city of Tyre. Her daughter was suffering from demonic oppression and she begged Jesus for help. His reply was that His Father sent Him only to help Jews and that it was "not right to take the children's bread and toss it to their dogs."[7] That's hardly politically correct stuff in these days of human rights and equal opportunities. The King of kings could get sued for that one! But what say we, Church, but that we let God be God and not try to reshape Him to fit into the mold of twenty-first century humanistic democracy?

Let's look at it through His lens. God's plan never was, nor ever will be, other than to bless His family. That's basically what Jesus expressed to this "outsider." But the Canaanite woman understood this, and in effect, responded, "That's right, but I know that this is the only place that I can get real help." At that, Jesus recognized her authentic heart cry, and in so many words, conceded, "It's obvious that you too are a part of the family; come on in out of the cold."

---

7.   Mt. 15:24-26.

Where Is the Body?

The salvation of Abraham's God always was and always will be "from the Jews," and no theological juggling past, present, or future can ever change that.

So to the half of the family that believed His message—and they were all Jews remember—Jesus the Jew told them to go into all the world, to all nations, that is to the *goyim*, and let them know that the King of the Jews is actually the King of everyone: "Welcome non-Jews to My Jewish family!" It is fascinating that His regal title, which we have just now used was actually endorsed, if not coined, by one less-than-virtuous Gentile named Pontius Pilate![8]

But the other half of the original family of Abraham, who could in no way comprehend this improbable Galilean carpenter as their Messiah, eventually got scattered to the ends of the earth. Moses warned them what could happen:

I will lay waste the land, so that your enemies who live there will be appalled. I will scatter you among the nations and will draw out My sword and pursue you. Your land will be laid waste, and your cities will lie in ruins (Leviticus 26:32-33).[9]

Now the sanctimonious Christian might be quick to judge that the scattering in A.D. 70 when Titus torched the temple, and again even more tragically in A.D. 132 when Emperor Hadrian leveled Jerusalem for a second time and changed the name of Judea to so-called *Palestine*, was initiated by divine retribution because the Jews "rejected Jesus." It is a very predictable presumption, except we won't exactly find it spelled out to that extent in God's Holy Book. Even should it dare be so, the Almighty has not given me or any other Gentile a license to judge on the matter.

The *Torah*, moreover, is replete with warnings to Israel against disobedience with the resulting curse of being driven from their land, the foremost pronouncement being against idolatry.[10] But we will not find a

---

8. Jn. 19:19-22.

9. See also Deut. 30:1-5.

10. Lev. 26:14-46; Deut. 28:15-68; in addition to numerous other references.

specific mention of the rejection of their Messiah listed among the potential sins for banishment from their heritage. Jewish soul searching today concedes that they were driven out of their homeland because of bitter jealousies, internecine rivalries, and infighting among themselves. Suffice it to say, the records would call it sin, and God sent them packing to the ends of the earth until His chosen time of ingathering. And that day seems to have now arrived.

But irony of ironies: We now behold the conceit of the Gentiles, who had seemingly snatched up the baton to forge on in the race. The Church has gone on many an enthusiastic crusade to try to garner the errant and unbelieving Jews into our sometimes buoyant, oft-times flagging, Christian harvest.

Firstly, touching on the semantics of the word *crusade*, those three despicable monuments to violence and hypocrisy were the less than brilliant Crusades launched by so-called Christians in the Middle Ages.[11] Notwithstanding, they were ideologically directed to "liberate" the Holy Land from the "infidel" Muslims (one would be quite put to the test to be forced to choose which camp was the more infidel); these ventures were so horrifically anti-Semitic that those Jews still residing in the area were bashed and battered, maimed and murdered regardless of which side was invading. So you can just imagine the sheer horror of inviting a neighborhood Jewish friend to come along with you to a "Gospel Crusade." The Jews know their history well. I would judge that your Jewish friend might just as soon be invited to a birthday party thrown for Adolph Hitler!

But secondly, on the prospect of gathering in those who have "strayed away," something has been fundamentally flawed with the Church's orientation of identity—and I specifically say *identity* rather

---

11. Between A.D. 1095 and 1250 so-called "Christian" Europe launched three violent Crusades. The atrocities of the first were directed against both Muslims and Jews alike. The second was primarily directed against Islam, but it was equally devastating to any Jews caught in its path. The violence of the third, which originated predominately from England, was most savagely thrust against the Jews. See *Encyclopedia Judaica*, Vol. 5 (Jerusalem: Keter Publishing House, Ltd., 1971), 1135-1141.

than *need*. If we know the Scriptures accurately, we have been adopted through our Messiah Jesus into *their* family, so how can we presume a successful inversion of the biblically defined circumstances by trying to reshape them to fit into a Gentile mold? The practicing Jew, or even the one who may not be quite so observant, senses enough of his roots of what his God planned for him to be—one of a people set apart—that an invitation from the Christian to deny his God-given heritage interests the ordinary Jew like finding a tarantula in his bed! The Church needs to learn to appreciate, not only a few more insights into Scripture, but also a lesson or two in sensitivity.

Clearly spelled out in Scripture is a somber warning to those of us in the Church who, as the original outsiders, are now adopted into the family of Abraham. In Romans 11 Gentile believers are unmistakably symbolized as wild olive branches grafted into Israel, the natural olive tree:

> *Do not boast over those* [broken off and discarded] *branches. If you do consider this: You do not support the root, but the root supports you* (Romans 11:18).

But hold it! Neither I nor indeed the Scriptures are saying that our Lord does not have something very beautiful to offer to His Jewish brothers and sisters. Nor are we saying that in many millennia of their struggle and suffering that they do not necessarily need the heartwarming personal intimacy and blessing that He will give them through His *Ruach Ha Kodesh.*

It is a well-worn principle that head knowledge isn't everything, but I would be prompt to add that stupidity isn't *anything*. Before we Gentiles dare open our mouths—not to mention our spiritual "fix-it" kits—we need to perceive who the Jews are in Abraham and how we ought to now relate to our far-away family, considering our own status of adoption by grace into their heritage through *their brother* and our Lord and Messiah.

Only then will we be in a position to love without pretense. Only then can we reflect the proper spirituality to present the warmth of an honest relationship with an often-offended, sometimes estranged member of the family. And only then will we evoke a genuine sort of envy[12] that would draw the family together under a Father's love and mutual forgiveness to all the kids—adopted or otherwise.

But "converting Jews" has long been an endemic passion by Christians of every stripe and persuasion. The word *convert*, or *conversion*, has its basic meaning in both Greek and Hebrew as to "turn back" or "turn away," and it is generally used in reference to a rejection of sin or a corrupt lifestyle. It is hardly meant to be used in a context of the rejection of one subculture over another or of a defection from one house of prayer to another. Sin is sin, culture is culture, and family patterns are family patterns. And even subconsciously approaching our Jewish brethren as if they were utter pagans is crass ignorance. We will have an even closer look at this in a later chapter.

So, depending on how Jewish he still is in his cosmic view, the Jew may find little to attract him in one of your church pews. But he could come to find great *benefit as a Jew in his own synagogue* as he contemplates a relevant encounter with his Messiah.

If one would carefully investigate, Saul's "conversion" is only termed as such in the section headings of your Bible and never in the text proper. Chapter and section headings are, of course, put there by Bible translators such as myself to assist the reader's grasp of the passage, but any such heading is hardly at the level of recognized Scripture canon. Regardless, Saul-come-Paul the apostle was indeed converted from sin, but he most certainly was not converted from his Jewishness. He was on frequent occasion ejected from the less flexible synagogues with the "left foot of no thanks," where those in charge preferred rigidity to revelation. Yet the synagogue was always preferred as the house of prayer for Paul the Jew. Moreover, it was the unmistakable place of worship for our Lord Himself.

But by now, nearly 2,000 years down the course of history, there seems little reassurance in that which I have outlined above that might suggest even the faintest hope for healing a tragically broken family. In

---

12.　Rom. 11:11,14.

the majority of Jewish-Christian relationships there is little love lost, not to mention all the hopelessly disintegrating fibers of a long-severed cord of mutual trust and understanding. The Judeo-Christian tradition of morality is quite certainly a shared concept that can still be indelibly recognized. But the practical reality of reaching across the breach to touch one another's souls is a broken dream.

The good news, however, is that the dream is God's and not man's. It was the Almighty who envisioned the plan, not Abraham. It will be the God of Abraham who will eventually effect all the difference *in the world*!

Almost unnoticed at first, in the latter half of the nineteenth century the Jews began to trickle back to their ancient homeland. Then on August 29, 1897, Dr. Theodore Herzl inaugurated the first World Zionist Congress in Basel, Switzerland. He wrote in his diary:

"If I were to sum up the Congress in one word, it would be this:
At Basel, I founded the Jewish State. If I were to say this today,
I would be greeted with universal laughter. In five years perhaps, and certainly in 50, everyone will see it."[13]

Herzl was correct on both counts. At the time, even many of his friends thought that he was a bit crazy in his absurd aspirations of a Jewish State. But precisely 50 years later, on November 29, 1947, the United Nations, in a rare moment of *goyim* sympathy for the tattered remnant of European Jewry who had escaped the horror of Hitler's genocide, voted to award the Jews with a minute sliver of what once had been their never-to-be-forgotten homeland. Then finally on May 14, 1948, Prime Minister David Ben Gurion arose to declare Israel to once more be a nation among the nations of the world. The exiled half of Abraham's family was headed home at last.

Nearly five million Jews have now returned to their homeland. It had been in 1967, exactly 70 years after Herzl's seemingly impossible vision, that the entirety of Jerusalem, the ancient City of David, fell back

---

13. *Israel God's Key to World Redemption* (Josephson: Bible Light Publications, 1974), 309.

A Fractured Family

into the hands of its God-appointed heirs through the miracle of the Six Day War. To kings and theologians alike, that which could never happen, happened! Sixteen of God's biblical prophets had predicted the eventual restoration of Jerusalem, and the faithful never let that dream fade away. God had never forgotten His promise to the original half of Abraham's family, who prayed at their Passover Seder's for 2,000 years: "Next year in Jerusalem."

And now what about the adopted Gentile half of Abraham's heritage? Unfortunately, not a few denied, scoffed, and explained away the miracle of the rebirth of Israel in 1948. It seems ironic that in 2,000 years the gift of skepticism had bounded from one side of the family to the other!

For any and all who are on the ground floor of perception into Jew and Gentile alienation, one is well aware that the cosmetic handshakes with business and society are an unreliable reflection of reality. Hardly will the United Nations ever produce a solution for the Arab-Israeli dichotomy, which is the classic demonstration of the immovable object being assailed by an irresistible force. Here we have two irreconcilable world views being buttressed by a colossal 4,000-year span of history. Nor could human design ever bring healing to the Jewish-Christian mistrust, which has a likewise formidable 2,000-year head start.

Nevertheless, quite like two millennia ago, there always seems to be a faithful, visionary remnant to be found. This time around, the strongest sensitivity to what is actually happening seems to be emerging among Bible-oriented *goyim* who have been awakened to appreciate their adoption into Abraham's far-flung heritage. As the last millennium begins its inevitable slide into history, the number of Gentiles who have been jolted to recognize the Christian Church's monumental debt to Israel are on a steady rise. There is a perceptible grassroots growth within the ranks of believers across all shades of Christian persuasion to come to unconditionally love and genuinely bless their newly recognized Jewish family.[14] Why? Perhaps you might tell me!

---

14. See Derek Prince, *Our Debt to Israel* (Ft. Lauderdale, FL: Derek Prince Ministries, 1985). Also, George Sweeting, *Our Debt to Israel* (Chicago: Moody Magazine, May/June 1996) 76.

There is indeed good news. It was neither demons, angels nor a clever president that promised Abraham a family "as numerous as the stars in the sky and as the sand on the seashore."[15] And if one has his eyes open, he will see that the impossible phenomena that are silently falling into place in this generation are being orchestrated by the only One who possibly could do so. His promises will be kept!

So it could well be that our fractured family might eventually be healed in spite of ourselves.

---

15.   Gen. 22:17.

Chapter 5

The Much-Misappropriated Mystery

One of my bedrock rules in the comprehension and subsequent interpretation of Scripture has been the "Two or Three Principle." The Law—the sacred Hebrew *Torah*—declares:

> *One witness is not enough to convict a man accused of any crime or offense he may have committed. A matter must be established by the testimony of two or three witnesses* (Deuteronomy 19:15).

A corollary is that in the case of an alleged murderer or other serious offender who has committed a crime that may warrant capital punishment, he dare not be sentenced to death on the word of only one witness. "On the testimony of two or three witnesses a man shall be put to death, but no one shall be put to death on the testimony of only one witness."[1] The principle spans the Scriptures.

Perhaps the most well-known New Testament application is Yeshua's teaching to have a basic quorum of at least "two or three" at

---

1.   Deut. 17:6; see also Num. 35:30.

your prayer meetings or you may not attain the priority attention you had hoped for.[2] He further cites the above *Torah* teaching in a confrontation with the Pharisees.[3] Paul the apostle likewise notes this rule as he underscores his credentials to the Corinthians[4] and applies it in dealing with accusations against errant church officers in his instructions to Timothy.[5] Finally, the author of the Book of Hebrews refers to this basic Mosaic principle in a challenge to continued confidence in God's faithfulness.[6]

So with that firmly established, would a God of Righteousness who requires a plurality of testimony in human affairs provide us with anything less in matters that He intends for us to clearly appropriate in our hearts and minds? I have discovered that throughout Scripture anything important, which our Creator God intends for us to pick up on, has been inspirationally repeated at least twice. But when it comes to concepts and revelations for which He wants to absolutely shake us into the significance of His message, He prompts the texts, lines, or even phrases to be reiterated well beyond His own "Two or Three Principle" just to make sure that He gets our undivided attention.

Unfortunately, even then He most often doesn't. I strongly surmise that the fault may well lie in our court instead of His! It never ceases to amaze me how the "religious" mentality can latch on to one isolated verse of Scripture and build a monument to legalism, while the oft repeated admonitions of the Almighty go unheard and unheeded.

It is fascinating that the most recurrent line[7] in New Testament Scripture is the simple but unforgettable statement of Jesus, which is repeated a total of 15 times:

---

2.   Mt. 18:19.

3.   Jn. 8:17.

4.   2 Cor. 13:1.

5   1 Tim. 5:19.

6.   Heb. 10:28.

7.   Obviously concepts using words such as *love, faith, sin,* and *obedience* are interspersed throughout the Scriptures with an even greater frequency, but our point is here being made with repeat phrases, lines, or whole texts.

34

The Much-Misappropriated Mystery

He who has ears, let him hear (Matthew 11:15).[8]

It brings to mind as well George Santayana's more contemporary corollary that those who fail to learn from the past "will be condemned to relive it." The tragic current condition of our greedy, competitive, materialistic, and hedonistic world starkly reminds us that humanity has neither had ears to hear then, nor have we learned by now. And we are living in a world condemned to go through it once more. I suggest that we continue our search for a *Body* with better ears than those around us.

A second, most-repeated verse, or variation of a verse, may also come as a bit of a surprise. There could be other contenders that I have overlooked, but nevertheless, when God tells us something ten times, we can presume that it might come relatively high on His list of importance. Come to think of it, that's exactly how many times He took hold of Pharaoh's ear—by means of ten plagues in the Book of Exodus.

Anyway, the One who spoke the lights of the heavens into existence on Day Four of creation, also left us a few notices on what to expect in case of a potential power outage somewhere along the line. In fact, He left us with ten notices:

> *I will show wonders in the heavens and on the earth, blood and fire and billows of smoke. The sun will be turned to darkness and the moon to blood before the coming of the great and dreadful day of the Lord* (Joel 2:30-31).[9]

That day will certainly be *great* for some of us, but quite *dreadful* for others. But note that this somber little announcement occurs a monumental ten times from Isaiah to Revelation. It may be an amazing study of human denial that, after God has put us on notice once for each plague He previously cast upon Egypt, there are still those professed believers

---

8. See also Mk. 4:9; Lk. 8:8; and several other occurrences in the Gospels, as well as Rev. 2–3; 13:9.

9. See also Is. 13:10; Joel 3:15; Amos 8:9; Mt. 24:29; Mk. 13:24; Lk. 21:25-26; Acts 2:20; Rev. 6:12; 8:12; 9:2.

who somehow manipulate reality to the point that they assume that today's blinking red warning lights could never possibly apply to them!

Another most prominent repetition includes the reply of Jesus when He was asked which of all the commandments was the most important:

> ... *"Hear, O Israel, the Lord our God, the Lord is one. Love the Lord your God with all your heart and with all your soul and with all your mind and with all your strength." The second is this: "Love your neighbor as yourself." There is no command-ment greater than these* (Mark 12:29-31).

The first half of His response was quoted from Deuteronomy chapter 6, which to this day still embodies the cornerstone of Jewish faith in the one and only God of Abraham. We will find it repeated in total four times, while the latter half of his declaration has an additional six references making a total of seven occurrences throughout both the Old and New Testaments.[10]

Then there is the controversial, often-theorized, much-misinterpreted, and frequently watered-down declaration of John the Baptist (no pun intended, but apply it if you like):

> *I baptize you with water, but He will baptize you with the Holy Spirit* (Mark 1:8).

The significance of this declaration is underscored all of seven times.[11]

All the above will carry—directly or indirectly—a great deal of significance throughout this book. We want to emphasize what God has emphasized, and not get tangled up with incidentals that do not have at least two or three witnesses to reinforce the point. I get really excited when we can climb up to as many as seven or more repeat texts, and

---

10. Deut 6:4-5; see also Lev. 19:18; Mt. 22:37-40; Lk. 10:27; Rom. 13:9; Mt. 19:19; Jas. 2:8.

11. Mt. 3:11; Mk. 1:8; Lk. 3:16; Jn. 1:26,31-33; Acts 1:5; 11:16.

particularly so when they have been plowed under for centuries by unwitting theologians.

So finally, to get to our main objective in this chapter, we have one more concept to focus upon which has also often been overlooked, mis-understood, misapplied, and misappropriated. It only occurs about ten times so we might forgive the experts for not getting it right. It happens to be the *mystery* unveiled to us in Ephesians 3, along with substantial support from the entire surrounding context.[12] Interestingly enough, the mystery comes to rest in Revelation Chapter 10 verse 7, which just might after all worm its way somewhere into our present time frame. All this carries significant weight since we will be obliged to make a repetitive application of the "Two or Three Principle" in our ensuing search for the *Body*.

So with this in mind, we note on at least three occasions from our preceding chapter that Yeshua had alluded to the basic premise that "sal-vation is of the Jews." This is not to say, of course, that He was not also allowing for the preordained expansion of the family that would ulti-mately inscribe the ends of the earth.

So let's have a look at how Paul the apostle conveyed it to the Gen-tile believers. We'll begin with the third chapter in his letter to the Eph-esians, which reads like this:

> *Surely you have heard about the administration of God's grace*
> *that was given to me for you, that is, the **mystery** made known*
> *to me by revelation, as I have already written briefly. In read-*
> *ing this, then, you will be able to understand my insight into the*
> ***mystery** of Christ, which was not made known to men in other*
> *generations as it has now been revealed by the Spirit to God's*
> *holy apostles and prophets* (Ephesians 3:2-5).

As a young believer years ago, I used to probe these lines along with the some ten other similar occurrences of the word *mystery* and get fired up with a charge of youthful curiosity for a good Alfred Hitchcock of

---

12.   Eph. 1:9; 3:3-4,6,9; see also Rom. 11:25; 16:25; Col. 1:26-27; 2:2; Rev. 10:7.

biblical vintage. But I was always a bit disillusioned. I could read it clearly enough. So God saves Jews, and God saves Gentiles. So what's the big mystery about that? My failure to grasp the relevance of the supposedly veiled secret was twofold.

Firstly, as a small boy my widowed mother taught me that Jesus loved me. I internalized that long before I ever heard that there was such a thing as a Jew, let alone a man named Abraham. My information was well apart from the true chronology of both Old and New Testament times.

Secondly, as I grew older and any Jewishness of the whole plan began to present itself to my reasoning, my interpretation was clouded with the subtle anti-Semitism that had seeped into Church mentality since Roman days and by now had been polished and refined to top quality evangelical standards. The blinders were firmly in place for many a year. That is, until I translated the Scriptures for the Waola tribespeople in the Highlands of Papua New Guinea. In sifting through those holy pages, the Holy Spirit—the Father's *Ruach Ha Kodesh*—began to put together why Paul's mystery, remained such a mystery, not only to me, but to those around me who somehow thought that they had made some sense out of it!

Let's get a little bit real. After all, the *Tanakh*, the Hebrew term that the Church fathers later renamed the Old Testament[13] was the only Scripture Jesus ever used. He quoted them and lived by them, and it is to the *Torah*, the first five books of the *Tanakh* that He referred to when He proclaimed:

> *I tell you the truth, until heaven and earth disappear not the smallest letter, not the least stroke of a pen, will by any means*

---

13. In some contexts the terminology *old* may have limited accuracy. The error generally encountered is the presumption that *old* means outdated. This is anything but truth. If one examines Hebrews 8:13, he will find that what has become obsolete is the animal blood sacrifice with the advent of a new Lamb. *Obsolete* is hardly an appropriate reference to the stories of the patriarchs, the majesty of the Psalms, and the accuracy of the prophets. It is far better that we refer to The Foundational Testament than to give rise to inference that these God-breathed pages are mere incidentals to be discarded.

disappear from the Law until everything is accomplished (Matthew 5:18).

Moreover, Paul charges Timothy to continue in the Scriptures that he learned from infancy. This is no less than our Old Testament which Paul advised Timothy would be *"able to make* [him] *wise* for salvation through faith in Christ Jesus."[14]

Nevertheless, with sheer disregard for the broad teaching of Scripture from Genesis to Revelation my "enlightened" Western heritage came up with the concept that God got so upset with the Jews when they didn't receive His Son that He decided to start over with a new entity called the Church. And the Church is presumed by many to be the *mystery* that Paul is referring to. The only mystery I can see, however, is why the Church today is so fragmented and why we haven't been able to make our Jewish brethren envious as the apostle Paul suggested that we do.[15] It seems all we've been able to do is make them angry!

That apostle Paul is describing the Church as a mystery is in itself a half truth—more precisely, something less than half. It is not what Paul presented; it is not what Jesus taught; it is totally out of sync with any or all of the prophets; and there is no implication throughout any other Scriptures in New Testament or Old that this might be so.

This anti-Semitic blooper has robbed the Church of much of her awareness of the immense depth of her heritage going through the Messiah Jesus an entire span of 4,000 years back to the richness of our roots in Abraham. And beyond Abraham is the eternal God of Abraham. It's a bit bigger than a nice brick church with a lovely steeple pointing to heaven. We might also be sensing the cosmic expanse of the God of Heaven Himself, and the kind of friendship with Him that Abraham had. Finally, this heretical rejection of our roots has caused untold heartache and devastation—not to mention spiritual blockage—to our other half of the Abrahamic family, the Jews.

---

14. 2 Tim. 3:15-16.

15. Rom. 11:11,13-14.

Where Is the Body?

Somehow our mentors of generations gone by seemed to overlook the words of Jeremiah:

This is what the Lord says, He who appoints the sun to shine by day, who decrees the moon and stars to shine by night, who stirs up the sea so that its waves roar—the Lord Almighty is His name. "Only if these decrees vanish from My sight," declares the Lord, "will the descendants of Israel ever cease to be a nation before Me" (Jeremiah 31:35-37).

Or what Isaiah proclaimed:

But Zion said, "The Lord has forsaken me, the Lord has forgotten me." "Can a mother forget the baby at her breast and have no compassion on the child she has borne? Though she may forget, I will not forget you! See, I have engraved you on the palms of My hands; your walls are ever before Me" (Isaiah 49:14-16).

A reawakened Mount Zion is beginning to stir not ten miles from where I create this chapter somewhere in the Judean hills just outside ancient Jerusalem. Most interesting!

So with these immovable stones from both the Old and New Testaments as our foundation, let us reexamine the aspects of apostle Paul's mystery as described in Ephesians 3:

This mystery is that through the gospel the Gentiles are heirs together with Israel, members together of one body, and sharers together in the promise in Christ Jesus (Ephesians 3:6).

This verse contains so much that has somehow been shooshed under the carpet with a genuine crafted Gentile broom labeled "MADE IN CONSTANTINOPLE"! First of all "heirs together with Israel" can spell nothing else than joint ownership; and "sharers together in the promise" means sharers together in the promise! One would think that it wouldn't require too much scholarship to get that correctly in place.

40

The Much-Misappropriated Mystery

And in addition we have the well-known—but I'm not sure how well comprehended—concept of the Body of Christ. More Scripture is in order. Backing up to Ephesians 2, we are told that our Messiah Himself bonded the two groups together—Jew and Gentile—into one body. He broke down the ethnically oriented and pagan barrier that separated them, and through His death and resurrection, He opened a door of love, forgiveness and Holy Spirit power to bring the two cultures together *"in one body"* to make *"one new man out of two."*[16]

Again this was hardly an afterthought. If we review the entire Genesis report of God's oft-repeated promise to His friend Abraham (six times at least), that he would be the channel of the Almighty's blessing upon all the peoples of the earth, we see the plan had been well programmed aeons beforehand.[17]

Finally, let's have a better look at that symbolic body. We already have noted one reference in Ephesians chapter 2 and another in chapter 3. The explicit clarity of the material discussed in those two texts should be good enough to satisfy our "Two or Three Witnesses" principle. But just for fun, let's follow the flow-on in that acclaimed unity chapter of Ephesians 4 emphasizing the validity of "one Lord, one faith, one baptism, one God and Father of all."[18] Ensuing in the same context of that particularly well-known text, we find in verse 4 we have one more reference to the *one Body* teaching of chapters 2 and 3; in verse 12 there is yet another point made of the *Body*, and finally, in verse 16 we have yet one more. Moreover, if one continues the search, he can find at least seven additional related texts throughout the New Testament, all of which are applicable to our above discussion.[19]

How many sermons have we heard from Chapter 4 in Ephesians to get the point across that brethren in the Christian arena ought to somehow lay down their swords and spears and make an effort to get on a bit

---

16.   Eph. 2:14-16; see also Eph. 3:6; 1 Cor. 12:13.

17.   Gen. 12:3; 15:5; 18:18; 22:18; 26:4; 28:14; Ps. 72:17; Acts 3:25; Gal. 3:8.

18.   Eph. 4:5-6.

19.   Rom. 12:5; 1 Cor. 10:17; 12:13,27; Eph. 1:22-23; Col. 1:18; 3:15.

better with one another? But, my good friend, it should by now not require a lightning bolt from heaven to comprehend that Paul the apostle did not write Ephesians Chapter 4 in the context of Baptists and Pentecostals, Catholics and Lutherans, or Methodists and Presbyterians. (I'm sorry if I missed your particular group, but I'll catch you in the next sentence.) It was penned by the anointing of God's Holy Spirit, not for petty infighting by those who certainly ought to know better, but for a far more celestial camp—for faithful Jew and believing Gentile programmed from the foundation of time to be divinely drawn together into one *Body!*

Perhaps the most telling text to put a capstone on our entire probe into Paul's mystery is this:

> *Therefore, remember that formerly you who are Gentiles by birth...remember that at the time you were separate from Christ, excluded from* **citizenship in Israel** *and* **foreigners to the covenants of the promise**, *without hope and without God in the world. But now in Christ Jesus, you who once were far away have been brought near through the blood of Christ* (Ephesians 2:11-13).

No honest student of this verse could ever twist it. Once you were out in the cold, but now through Messiah Jesus you have been *included as citizens of the nation.* The Church has in no way *replaced* the promised family to Abraham; rather, we have *entered* it. Paul says, "I have a *mystery*—a secret for you Gentiles—that has been tucked away from view for centuries on end. Through trust in our Jewish Messiah, you one-time idolatrous, polytheistic pagans are now also entitled to *citizenship in Israel*—full participation, full rights to the promises, and full adoption into the family of Abraham."

I have heard it incompletely taught—and I'm sure you have too—that the Gentile Church happens to be the Body of Christ. Of course that is what the Scriptures do say, but they also say *much more*, which we have endeavored to fill in above. But then certain other teaching also goes to present that in contrast to the *Body*, the remnant of Jews to be saved—in the Millennium or some such shadowy time—will be the Bride.

The Much-Misappropriated Mystery

Now both of the above are about as much theological hocus pocus as you would want to run into in any one day. There are only four possibly applicable references to the Bride of the Messiah in the New Testament.[20] The major text which is in Revelation Chapter 21, symbolizes the Bride as the New Jerusalem prepared as a "bride beautifully dressed for her husband."[21] In the metaphor this exotically celestial city just happens to have 12 gates, each gate inscribed with the names of one of the 12 Tribes of Israel. But on the foundations of the gates, the allegory depicts the names of the 12 apostles, which are exclusively associated with the Church—those believers in Yeshua as the Messiah. Isn't that interesting! It is strangely reminiscent of that *sharing together* concept so clearly outlined in our above texts in Ephesians. And what's more, both groups seem to be solidly, equally and inseparably infused into what the Bible refers to as the *Bride of Christ.*

Now in every culture I have ever been in—and I have been associated with more than a few—brides are customarily associated with bodies. In the highlands of Papua New Guinea and other areas of the Pacific, brides with stronger bodies are preferred to make better workers in the home or in the garden. It is hardly a degrading or discriminatory choice, as some equal opportunists from the West might naïvely suppose. Rather it's a mutual family understanding for an optimum partnership in the household. However, in some western cultures, a slimmer variety of women is courted for perhaps a variety of reasons, one of which may even include a bit of prestige value for a male with a shrinking ego. And still in other cultures, a slimmer bride is potentially a sickly partner. She requires a few more kilos to stay healthy! Nor is the concept of a body—robust or petite—hardly marginalized in the less-than-platonic bride in the Song of Solomon. It is ludicrous to propose that the Bride of Christ and His Body are anything but one and the same concept.[22]

---

20. Rev. 21:2; see also Jn. 3:29; Rev. 21:9; 22:17.

21. Rev. 21:9-14.

22. In Ephesians 1:22-23, Paul does make reference to the Church as Christ's Body, but in the following three chapters of the same epistle, he makes it indisputably clear that the Gentiles are not the exclusive body but an inclusion into that body. Refer again to the warning of this anti-Semitic temptation to reject the Jews out of hand in Romans 11:17-21.

Where Is the Body?

It brings to mind the story of one diminutive little man named Ibisub who I first met in the hinterlands of Papua New Guinea in about 1963. We had entered the Waola Tribe as Bible translators, and in those early days of emergence from the Stone Age most men had more than one wife. But little old Ibisub did not. In fact, he did not even have one wife. He had been a poor fellow all his life and never had accumulated enough pigs and pearl shells to pick up a fair bride in his day. As he got older, he ultimately discovered another hapless have-not in much the same predicament. The two unfortunates eventually pooled their pigs and their shells to jointly bargain for an older widow to dutifully tend to their domestic requirements. Well by the time we arrived on the scene, the luckless lady had long died, as had also Ibisub's co-husband. But this little old man's benign notoriety stemmed from his unique distinction among the Waola tribesman of having had only half a wife!

Though my illustration is hardly from the Scriptures, the principle is superb. Could someone please explain to me how our Messiah could possibly return for half a bride?

So just exactly where is she now? *Where is the Body?*

Chapter 6

The Paganization of Christianity

So with all that Scripture to enlighten, whatever happened to the basic understanding within the Church on the very simple *"one Body"* concept—consisting of both Jew and Gentile—so clearly spelled out most particularly in the Book of Ephesians? How did the Church ever get off on the tangent that she and she alone was a new spiritual entity in her own right without an obligation to her original Hebraic roots?

Do we so misinterpret Paul's confrontation with *some* of his Jewish brethren that we take the liberty to dismiss his very own counterbalancing comments in all of Romans 9, 10, and 11, including his distinct warning against Gentile spiritual pride? His also was the well-known body metaphor from First Corinthians chapter 12 that the hand dare not say to the foot, "I do not need you"!

Certainly there were not insignificant tensions beginning with the controversies over the claims of Jesus and the authenticity of His teaching, not to mention the contention over His crucifixion and resurrection. These conflicts heightened in Peter's initial contact with—and corresponding conversion of—Cornelius the Gentile,[1] and extended into

---

1.   Acts 10–11.

45

Where Is the Body?

Paul's frequent confrontation with his fellow Jews in the Diaspora. A council of the disciples meeting at one stage in Jerusalem circulated their conclusions that any new Gentile proselytes into the "family" might be excused from most aspects of ceremonial Law.[2] Even though this ruffled not a few feathers among many of the less flexible sons of Abraham, there had not yet been a total rift between the God-fearing observant Jew and those—both Jew and Gentile—who had come to recognize Yeshua as their Messiah. It must be recognized that a total cleavage of these two variant views, with their eventually well-drawn battle lines of animosity and distrust, were not yet irreparably rent apart until almost 300 years after New Testament times.

Ironically, one of the most paradoxical differences of the two groups has been given little if any notice by Christian theologians, unless it be by an unconscious inversion syndrome of accusing Jews of the exact blind spot so prevalent among their accusers. That disparity is no less than legalism. But hardly is it the "Mosaic legalism" that is the differentiation. Quite the contrary, it is the more hypocritical "Christian legalism" that had surfaced in the longer term outgrowth of Christianity. Insight into the matter is one of those gems I picked up doing my "graduate studies" on the backside of the mountain in a once Stone Age setting. Let's drop into the classroom for "Legalism 101," one of the blue ribbon courses "offered" at the "Waola Institute of Human Behavior"!

When we first moved in among the Waola tribespeople in the rugged Papua New Guinea Highlands in the early 1960's for linguistic analysis and Bible translation, we were eager to share with them the immense value of a positive relationship with the one true God. To my amazement, they informed us that this was no big news. Their ancestors had already known of Him. His name, in fact, was *Sabkakl Yinaol Isi Hobao Sao*—"The One Important Son From Above." He was the Good Spirit and was reported to give their men a bit of assistance as they went off to battle with an enemy tribe. But aside from that He had little relevance for their daily distresses. Rather, their acute miseries stemmed from the very real demonic forces who ruled their livelihood, struck their children with disease, threatened

---

2.   Acts 15.

their own lives with untimely death, and by and large, were the controlling forces of every phase of their being from devastating curses to the productivity of their gardens.

Our presentation of the God of the Bible, therefore, became much easier: "The 'One From Above' of whom you have already heard is far superior to these deceptive demon powers that threaten your very existence. If you will indeed look to Him, He will very adequately tend to these treacheries that torment you." Well, they did. And He did!

There was just one small problem. In their initial transfer of allegiance, it soon became clear that they had indeed switched deities, but they had failed to make the corresponding psychological shift in the manner of *worshiping* those deities! And that was a problem, because their former demonic masters had approached them as a demanding and oppressive enemy. The new "Preferred Alternative" was coming to them as a caring and covering Father. The inadvertent result of their oversimplified switch was, however, a super-legalistic approach to a God that neither desired nor asked for appeasement. We would hardly suggest that the Almighty has no interest whatsoever in respect and obedience. That is ludicrous. But His requirement for the Waolas—and for all the rest of us—is first and foremost the awareness of a Father who cares, a God who forgives, and a Savior that has already paid the bill.

Simply stated, the God of the Universe has made Himself available to establish a close and personal relationship with His family. And it follows that a personal relationship gives rise to mutual sensitivities and reciprocal responsibilities. Yet these by sheer reason would be quite spontaneous in contrast to legal obligations. And it follows further that the greater the intimacy, the more fervent are the instinctive responses. This is a far cry from doing the right things so that God will like us. If we really understand what the Bible is actually telling us, His acceptance of those who yearn to be His "friends" is without question. It is a biblical verity that "…He chose us in Him before the creation of the world…."[3]

---

3.   See Ephesians 1:4-5 for an example.

Where Is the Body?

But there's much more to this a little closer home than the wild and woolly Papua New Guinea Highlands of 1960 vintage. If we have any scholarly appreciation at all of apostle Paul's letter to the Romans,[4] our faith in our Messiah begins not with some sentimental away-in-a-manger advent to Bethlehem, nor even His dramatic stand-up-and-be-counted introduction by John the Baptist. It all starts with Abraham.

In Chapter 1, we noted that one of the less savory aspects of Abraham's old hometown of Ur-come-Babylon was the multiplicity of pagan deities. So when the Lord of all creation called upon Abraham to move out for the purpose of producing a unique family, it wasn't just the real estate that God wanted changed. "Get rid of all those idols, Abraham, because there's only One of Me, and on that basis, and that basis alone, we can work together." So the tin gods of Babylon were out, *El Shaddai* was in, and God started building a faith relationship with His new family founder right then and there. And from then on, if anything was anathema to the obedient, observant Hebrew it was idolatry:

Hear, O Israel! The LORD is our God, the LORD alone (Deuteronomy 6:4).[5]

To summarize what we have detailed in our opening chapters, Abraham was called to build a very special family of promise. Then some 600 years later, Moses was chosen and groomed to teach that family what right living was all about. And then again after some two millennia more had passed, the Father God of Abraham sealed the promises to His family with His ultimate purpose. He filled a select human body with His very own *Ruach Ha Kodesh* to finalize His Abrahamic covenant with an everlasting sacrifice of human blood, willingly surrendered by His own Divine Spirit. The New Covenant was anything but a reversion to polytheism with the advent of a "new god" on the block. Rather the One and Only God of all the Universe chose from the beginning of time to replace the temporal animal sacrifices with a lasting sacrifice of His eternal design. He involved

---

4.   Particularly Romans 3:9 through 5:2.

5.   From *The TANAKH: The New JPS Translation According to the Traditional Hebrew Text.* Copyright 1985 by the Jewish Publication Society. Used by Permission.

Himself totally by His Spirit within His chosen suffering servant of clay, who we simultaneously have come to know as the Son of Man.

Then as we recounted in Chapter 4, the family of Abraham eventually fragmented. A major segment of the family could never agree to the authenticity of the new Lamb, and for whatever other reasons there may or may not have been, they were eventually dispersed into exile. The Father put them on hold in other far-off lands while He began to work in earnest with the other side of the household with something Paul the apostle later identified as "the fullness of the Gentiles."[6]

But we must take careful note that the dispersion was hardly one-sided. Those who were less than impressed with the newly proclaimed Messiah were not at all alone in seeking out new neighborhoods. These were the days that all Jews eventually became *persona non grata* in Jerusalem and environs. If we recall after the resurrection, Jesus charged the believing segment of the faithful to "go and make disciples of all *nations*" [read: Gentiles][7] with His personal invitation for any and all to become His disciples. Never was there a question among His early followers that this was anything but an invitation for inclusion into Abraham's family of promise. It is becoming increasingly acknowledged in Jewish scholarship today that except for His frequent reference to God as His Father and His refusal to deny His role as the Messiah, Jesus taught nothing that any good orthodox rabbi would not also have taught then or now.[8]

So it was that everyone and everything Jewish had to leave town. Some departed in gloom and tragic despair. Others, a bit more upbeat, headed out with a message. But once again, we must underline, they were all considered to be *one and the same family.*

---

6.   Rom. 11:25 KJV.

7.   Mt. 28:19.

8.   Arthur W. Kac, *Are Jews Changing Their Attitude Toward Jesus?* (Grand Rapids: Baker Book House, 1980), 20. Also see Ken Burnett, *Why Pray for Israel?: The Jewishness of Jesus by a Jew* (Basingstoke, Hants, U.K.: Marshalls Paperbacks), 194.

Where Is the Body?

But then some three centuries down the line, enter Emperor Constantine. Both Jew and believing Gentile had suffered enormously under pagan Rome. Under allegiance to the one and only God of Heaven, the faithful of the family would far rather choose torture and death than to yield either heart or knee to the fraudulent lordship of Caesar. The blood of the martyrs has always been known to be the seed of the Church. Nor did persecution ever daunt the Jew. It has always drawn the Jews together as a people, and they have been even the more determined in faithfulness to their God from it. Rome, it seems, never did have the best track record to daunt the spirits of the true believers—Jew or Gentile. So if you can't beat this crowd, join them. Constantine ultimately joined the Church.

Now if there was still a thread of communication at that point between the traditional Jew and the Gentile believer in Yeshua, Constantine fixed all that.[9] He relished the Jews as did Pharaoh, Nebuchadnezzar, Haman, or any model Roman Emperor for that matter. He saw to it that the evolving Christianity was quite sanitized from anything bearing witness to our Jewish roots and promptly set out to rewrite the Sunday Morning Church Bulletin.

In fact, he rearranged a lot of things. He pulled the "rabbit out of the hat" as it were, and instituted a heathen Easter holiday—complete with fertility symbols of eggs and bunnies—to replace the biblically prescribed Passover. He revamped another pagan season to commemorate the birthday of Jesus, which "just happens" to be in December around the time of the historic Jewish celebration of Chanukah, but "Caesar forbid" that anything Jewish might contaminate the festivities! It is more likely that Yeshua was born in September during the celebration of the Feast of Tabernacles, which has even greater Jewish significance, but for our

---

9.   "With its spread among the gentiles, the pagan characteristics of Christianity gained in influence, and after Constantine the Great and the adoption of Christianity as the official religion of the Roman Empire, the traditional Hellenistic-pagan forms of civic, social, and cultural anti-Semitism merged with the specifically Christian theological motifs to form an amalgam that has left a tragic legacy to history" (*Encyclopedia Judaica*, Vol. 5, [Jerusalem: Keter Publishing House, Ltd., 1971]), 511.

The Paganization of Christianity

Roman emperor, that would have been barbecue to the bonfire. To be sure the Sabbath had to go. So now we have Sun Day, which he substituted as a bit of a sop to placate one of his original masters when this new "Jesus-god" began to usurp the limelight. Never hurts to keep those fingers crossed, you know!

Well, some of the Church has awakened a bit to this sacrilege with not a few attempts to re-paper the walls in the House of the Lord. Sunday has of late been more decently decreed as "The Lord's Day," and Easter is now more reverently known to many as "Resurrection Day." Not too bad for starters!

Personally, I don't get too bent out of shape in learning that we have inherited some tragically poor terminology or get overly shaken about the skeletons in our theological closets. I have the same Friend that Abraham did, and He helps me get these things sorted out one at a time.

But all these things are peanuts compared to the biggest booboo in the legacy of our illustrious "Christian" emperor. Let's relate our anecdote of the Waola tribespeople from earlier in the chapter together with probably his most damaging fiasco of all.

Quite unlike Abraham—and it would be quite helpful at this point to be thoroughly familiar with chapter 4 of the book of Romans— Constantine never dispensed with his old idols. He added a new "Jesus," as it were, to his shelf of tin gods, and repentance took on the misconstrued meaning of merely turning to a new system. As the exiled half of Abraham's heritage once more tottered in obedience to a Father who banished them to the ends of the earth, the "adopted" side of the family also began a downhill slide from which the Church still smarts. We yet do battle to be fully free from Rome's paganized approach to faith. Jesus was never intended to become a *second* god, but He was a love expression of the one and only Lord God of Deuteronomy 6:4 sent to redeem His family—until this infamous emperor shifted the goal posts!

How? Constantine presumed an attitude toward Jesus not unlike service to the other pagan deities to whom Rome bowed down. You *do the right things* to catch the eye of the gods. If you *do the wrong things*,

51

the gods frown. With this new religion—and it was a religion, not an Abrahamic type of relationship—to appease this new god (or was it three new gods?) you still employed the proper articles of worship, wore the right robes, effected an acceptable appearance, followed correct procedures, and gave prescribed offerings. As a matter of fact, money would do just fine this time around! And then, if you did it right and the offerings were sufficient, you just might find favor in the eyes of this new "Jesus-god." And so it was that the Church began to develop over time— we certainly would not infer that it happened overnight. "Christian Law" came to replace an increasingly distasteful Law of Moses.

To be sure, all the above forms of practice can be related in one way or the other to the *Torah* teaching that God gave to Moses for the Children of Israel. But the great watershed is, *Why do you do what you do?* We recognized in Chapter 2 that an observant Jew does not keep the Law to *become a Jew* but because *he is a Jew*. He does it because this is the pattern of living his God has ordered. He is not a *mamzer*. In fact he is most legitimate. He knows who his Father is. And he lives to obey his Father God.

The converse is, when you have done the right things, your god will accept you—perhaps? If you have done well enough, He will. But have you done well enough…? Can you ever do well enough? This mentality makes the deity out to be a master and not a Father; a pay clerk and not a God. This is a totally pagan approach through and through. It is a world apart from an Abraham-like relationship with your Friend. And never the twain shall meet!

Thank you, Emperor Constantine, for using your powerful pagan influence to lead the Church to assume that when they do the right things, pray the right prayers, and sing the right songs, the gods will like them! That was neither the righteous road of faith in your day, nor is it a valid faith—a credible Christianity—today.

But I offer a genuinely truthful thanks to the insights of the many godly reformers who have seen to it that "Christian Law" has improved a tad over the last four centuries. Nevertheless, law is still law. And unfortunately, Constantine's non-biblical approach to God still muddles many of us. Not unlike the Waolas' initial attempts to appease God, he infected the Church with the very same pagan tactics toward things holy. I'm afraid the Church unwittingly sat down on the Emperor's pet porcupine, and unfortunately we're still pulling out the quills today!

We must grasp this. If a Jew does not keep the Law to *become a Jew* but *because he is a Jew*, how can we even dare assume that one must pursue "Christian law" to become a believer? It ought to be a bedrock conclusion that a relationship with the God of Abraham—or the God and Father of Yeshua for that matter—is a revelation and not a procedure!

Even if the "Christian Laws" be reduced to four, and they are readily recognizable to be the four most *"spiritual laws"* in the Book, one is still surfing the "Scripture net" with the wrong address code! I would hardly say that you cannot find God in any measure by this mini-legalistic procedure. That would again be to revert to the paganistic mentality that there is the dichotomy of the right rules and the wrong techniques. Not so. Most likely it is that the Almighty in His infinite grace has found you, rather than that you have finally found Him!

Does this confuse you? If so, we must yet award a few more phony bonus points to the now infamous emperor. Of course, there is atonement; of course, there is forgiveness; of course, there is a righteousness by faith. But all this and more has been well in place long before you and I ever arrived on the scene. Is Almighty God a reality? Faith is not something you *do*. Faith is Someone you see with spiritual eyes.

What I *am*, I *become*.
I *do not become* in order to *be*.

By definition, I adhere to my Christian morality and principles not *to become* a Christian, but because I *am* a Christian. And those two concepts are worlds apart! One is the pagan mentality of serving a god-master to get off the hook. The other follows the relationship Abraham began when he looked up in unlimited obedience and said as it were: "I read You loud and clear." Church, we must return to our Abrahamic roots of a relationship to a Friend, a kinship to a Daddy, an *Abba* to put His arms around us, rather than a paganistic and legalistic approach to just be doing enough to keep Him off our backs!

And we Christians are the "pure" believing ones who have long accused the Jews of being legalistic! I'm sorry, but this is a tragic gap of *goyim* insight into many a devout Jew's relationship with his God. There may even be a mite we could learn from some of the faithful from among our Jewish family! I am hardly suggesting that there is no need of a Lamb, or that this is the extent of all what a Jew's relationship with his God could or even will be. This is not so. There is much yet tucked away in the Book for valuable insights into these matters, but at the moment we'll have to put it on hold until a later chapter.

Our Waola friends with whom we began our discussion, have long since turned a corner and gotten it right. And in the entire process, our once Stone Age mentors have left us with a truly invaluable insight. I can never profitably serve the Almighty by altering my lifestyle so that God will *accept me*. That acceptance and that forgiveness had been long established from the foundations of time and was subsequently ratified in blood on Golgotha.

In summary, the Church as a whole needs to return to an Abraham-ic quality of faith. His offspring are bonded in a relationship to a Father, not a legal burden as so many of the uninformed have stereotyped. And thank you, Waola Highlanders, for the valuable object lesson from your former pagan worldview—the *wrong way* to approach the one and only *right* God.

And last of all, Emperor Constantine, you can go now. We won't require your services any more. And please do not forget to take all your legalistic pagan baggage with you. We don't need that either!

Chapter 7

Porcupine Quills

It's amazing that it has never occurred to many otherwise knowledgeable people that the now-turbulent Palestinian-Israeli confrontations did not initially originate in our times with the advent of terrorist-come-statesman Yasser Arafat's Palestine Liberation Organization in 1964.[1] Nor did the Arab-Israeli conflagration in general even begin with Israel's Declaration of Independence and fledgling statehood in 1948, incurring the wrath and venom of seven Arab armies who had sworn by the name of Allah that they would never let it happen.[2] And very few of my readers would have the tenure of world awareness to recall the Arab massacres of the Jews of Hebron in 1929 and 1936,[3] spilling Jewish blood over the streets of the city which was first founded by Abraham some 4,000 years back into history.

---

1. Samuel Katz, *Battleground: Fact and Fantasy in Palestine* (New York: Bantam, 1973), 138-148.

2. *History from 1880*, Israel Pocket Library from *Encyclopedia Judaica* (Keter Publishing House Ltd., Jerusalem, 1971), 91,124-125. For the most thorough coverages of the War of Independence, see Collins and Lapierre, *O Jerusalem!* (Hemel Hempstead, U.K.: Simon & Schuster, 1972).

3. *Encylopedia Judaica*, Vol. 8 (Keter Publishing House, Ltd., Jerusalem, 1971), 235.

Where Is the Body?

So what else is new? As we already well know, anti-Semitism was hardly invented by Chairman Arafat and the Palestinians. Nor is the constant anti-Israeli propaganda, slander and oft-subtle barrage of innuendoes by the gamut of an antagonistic press a phenomena of our times. But even at that, one must concede, that the electronic noose does seem to be getting ever tighter with time. But from the beginning, just what was Pharaoh's problem with his self-proposed labor pool of rag-tag Hebrew slaves? Or what virus chewed on old Haman's ego, or Nebuchadnezzar's, or the Greeks' or Romans' or Adolph Hitler's? Doesn't it seem strange to you that such a minute world minority can have such hatred directed against them?

There are only two answers. The first one is that those Jews truly must be a despicable lot, just like all those nice guys in the paragraph above were trying to tell us. But that answer has some problems. How can it be that this allegedly sinister race has produced ten percent of the world's Nobel prize winners in science and medicine when they represent less than one half of one percent of the entire world population! "Undoubtedly, it's a diabolical trick; those Jews are clever you know!" the bitter bigots would tell us. So let's try one more question to forever flatten that first less-than-brilliant response. Just how can it be that these people feature so prominently in your Bible, with God picking one of them to be your Messiah?

The alternative answer is that something different is going on here. Shall we begin to get a bit real? No sooner had the Almighty put His arm around Abraham than the rest of the world started getting jealous. And I have yet to find a culture in the world where jealousy is a glowing virtue.

So whether the remainder of society likes it or not, it appears that the Jewish nation is Almighty God's footprint on the human race to effect His purposes from the beginning of the plan to the culmination of the age. They are not His spoiled goody-goody saints, but they do represent His select cross section of humanity—programmed to do a job of eternal destiny. It might come as a complete surprise to the anti-Semite, but as in every cultural diversity on the globe, stereotyping is not a terribly intelligent exercise. And like any good protective parent, God says, "Don't touch My kids! If they're naughty, I'll take care of the problem and I alone. You touch My kids and you're in trouble with Me!" It has been a principle throughout Scripture that God uses the enemies of Israel to discipline His people, but turns again to severely punish those who have dared to touch the "apple of His eye."[4]

On the other hand, being on *El Shaddai's* stage has not always been the easiest, as in the classic comment in *Fiddler on the Roof* by the delightful Tevye who lifts one eye to heaven and says, "I know we're Your Chosen People, but couldn't You choose someone else just once in a while?"

Some may not agree. Even many of my very dear Jewish friends may shake their heads profusely to shed off the stigma that the world has so erroneously assumed and so ignominiously slung upon them. But may I remind you that we are not here to take a poll on what may or may not be "politically correct" in this decade or the next. Those who find this hard to accept will find that they are at loggerheads with what is increasingly regarded as an outdated and politically flawed Bible. However, this is not the case; the plan proves out to be most logical, and the watercourse of history that follows it, quite realistic.

In His own wisdom, the God of Heaven put His finger on the family of Abraham to carry out His divine purposes in a prototype of humanity. Perhaps it is not even the Jews that the world so despises, but rather the nations are unwittingly trying to get back at their Creator in the cheapest way they know how. Humankind is terrified of that "divine finger," and moreover, they shake their own fists at the hand that would bend their wills to effect His authority and all His control in their otherwise self-styled agendas.

But now we are seeing even the Church—that select fellowship of saints that was preordained to be grafted into the family of Abraham and inherit the promises—falling into line with the Caesars of their day to condemn the "despicable" Jew. "Constantine the convert" was only one more link in a long chain of a humanity that despises any really sovereign intrusion into his personal life—his "human rights" as it were. Now 16 centuries after Constantine, our humanistic world has become awash in an ocean of political democracy, and the tenor of the times has likewise more than watered down much of the Church: "If I don't like your *gospel*, I'll move across the street for one that suits me better."

---

4. Deut. 32:10; Jer. 12:14-17; Obad. 1:10; Zech 2:8-9.

But for our particular purposes in these pages, may we continue a focus on the world's use of the God of Abraham's originally chosen family as an unwitting scapegoat in an overall rejection of the Father's authority. And the Church, in letting an Abrahamic type of relationship slide into a system of religious observance, has sadly joined the queue.

As we noted previously, the early Messianic believers in Yeshua—that first generation of Jews who genuinely recognized their Messiah—suffered for their stand. What ultimately began to be recognized as the Church—the *ecclesia*—faced pressure and persecution from all sides. The wound between the traditional Jew and the believer in the newly discovered Messiah—whether he be Jew or Gentile—had hardly healed. Rome was even more violent in her attack. Until, of course, Emperor Constantine raised his head. At that point persecution of the "recognized" Church became a bit of history. An axiom we must never lose sight of: *The further the Church became severed from her Jewish roots, the less was her persecution!*

Those days after Constantine the Great were dark days, with an emerging hierarchy that not only questioned but usurped the authority of a Father who was presumably far too distant, if not far too busy with other more pressing matters of celestial significance. Anyway, by now He had new "staff" who were becoming increasingly learned in how operating such a magnificent cache of spiritual power might be better handled! And so it was that the times became blacker and even blacker as humanity slid more and more deeply into the centuries we now call the Dark Ages.[5] But no soul suffered more bitterly in those black days than the Jew—God's pre-selected Family.

This was the era when the Jew began to be officially decried, maligned, and cursed, accused by so-called Christians of poisoning the wells[6] and even of being the perpetrators of the deadly bubonic plague that wiped out about one-third of Europe's population between 1348 and

---

5. The Dark Ages spanned an era of over 1,000 years from approximately A.D. 300 to A.D. 1500. See Murray Dixon, *The Rebirth and Restoration of Israel*, (Chichester, England: Sovereign World, 1988).

6. Martin Luther, "On the Jews and their Lies," (1543), translated by Martin H. Bertram, edited by Franklin Sherman: Volume 47, pages 121-306 of Jaroslav Pelikan and Helmut T. Lehmann, *Luther's Works*, (Philadelphia: Fortress Press and St. Louis: Concordia Publishing House, 1962-1974), as cited by David H. Stern, *Restoring the Jewishness of the Gospel* (Jerusalem: Jewish New Testament Publications, 1988), 64.

Porcupine Quills

1349.[7] Jews were violently beaten, driven out of town, and frequently murdered. No, it was not a reincarnated Herod or a Haman come back to life. This time around it was a purported "righteous" cleansing at the vicious behest of a regime that sanctimoniously laid hold of the claim to be God's anointed agents! Is it any wonder the days were dark?

For that matter, does anyone presume that the utter decimation of Hitler's Third Reich after World War II had nothing to do with the inhumane genocide of His Chosen Nation? Or that the downward spiral in the Western world of materialism-come-Sodom-and-Gomorrah since World War II was a prize from the Almighty for defeating Hitler? Indeed! What happened to our brains, and where are our Bibles?

"It is mine to avenge; I will repay," says the Lord (Romans 12:19b).

But if vengeance is His, severe nearsightedness must certainly be the birthright of multitudes of those who so carelessly call themselves by His name! Perhaps the Church in the West has forgotten—or perhaps they never even knew—that when Hitler was unleashing his murderous insanity throughout Europe, Western governments were all the while limiting immigration for many Jews who were so desperately trying to escape the Nazi hell that had engulfed Europe.[8]

So now for a few other of those porcupine quills. Four legacies of Constantine's "conversion" might be spelled out as something less than divine dividends to the Church over the ages.

Of course in those dark early days of ignorance and illiteracy, it was hardly much of a trick to raise a barbaric, blood-thirsty anti-Semitic crowd. "The Jews killed Jesus. They killed our God! Let's go get a few of them to even the tally!" The satanic barbarism of the hour was beyond all comprehension of morality, decency, and truth. An awareness of a God of righteousness and His Holy Book lay buried in the impenetrable

---

7.   Michael Brown, *Our Hands Are Stained With Blood* (Shippensburg, PA: Destiny Image Publishers, 1992), 60-61.

8.   For shocking reports of callous insensitivity to the Jewish plight at the hand of the Nazis, see Unfulfilled Promise: Rescue and Resettlement of Jewish Refugee Children in the United States 1934-45 (Juneau, AL: Denali Press, 1990), 10-23. See also Benjamin Netanyahu, *A Place Among the Nations* (New York: Bantam, 1993), 70-73, and for reports of British culpability, see Ramon Bennett, *Saga* (Jerusalem: Arm of Salvation, 1993), 152, 156-158.

shadows of ignorance and superstition. And tragedy of tragedies, blasphemy of blasphemies, it was all done in His name!

In a unique turnabout, Vatican II made history in 1965 with the official recognition that although due respect is to be shown to the faith of all men, the Jew in particular has a special relationship with the Church that followers of other world religions do not share. "Nevertheless, the Jews still remain most dear to God because of their fathers, for He does not repent of the gifts He makes, nor of the calls He issues."[9] Would to God—the God of Abraham—that this recognition fans to the extremities of the Christian faith.

And it is with an overdue satisfaction that, after centuries of pain and humiliation to our Jewish brethren, Pope John Paul II came out with an unprecedented statement in his 1998 Easter message, declaring that, "the Jewish people have 'been crucified by us for too long,' adding that 'not they, but we, each and every one of us' are responsible for Christ's crucifixion, 'because we are all murderers of love.' "[10] But for over 16 centuries pitiful ignorance, bloodshed, and malicious pain held sway.

But it was hardly the Catholic arm of the Church alone that inherited the stains of Constantine's "conversion." Throughout the Protestant Church there eventually swept the devastating deception known as "Replacement Theology," which even today, otherwise enlightened evangelicals still firmly clasp to their bosoms. It is with utter ignorance of the Scriptures, to be sure. This preposterous theft of Jacob's birthright, has been so thoroughly dealt with in other publications that we need to add little additional rebuttal of it here.[11] Suffice it to say that the theory presents a deceptive manipulation of certain Scripture texts coupled with a

---

9.   Vatican Council II, *The Declaration on the Relationship of the Church to Non-Christian Religions* (Vatican City, Rome, 1965), *The World Book Encyclopedia*, Vol. 20, 1976.

10. "The Jews have been crucified by us for too long." *Jerusalem Post International Edition*, April 12, 1998.

11. Jesma O'Hara, *The Day of Restoration for Israel and the Church*, (International Christian Embassy Jerusalem: Nambour, Qld. 1998), 32-40. See also Henry Bettenoon, *Documents on the Christian Church* (London: Oxford Univ. Press, 1963); Murray Dixon, *The Rebirth and Restoration of Israel* (Chichester: Sovereign World, 1988); Rabbi Yechiel Eckstein, *What Christians Should Know About Jews & Judaism* (Waco: Word, 1984); Marvin Wilson, *Our Father Abraham* (Grand Rapids: Erdmans, 1991).

total disregard of others. The postulation is that God has quite finished with the Jews as a bad "first try," which would seem to give allegiance to a deity capable of making a mistake! But this god is certainly no quitter so he eventually ends up going for a rerun with an entirely new Gentile entity called the Church. However, this neo-Scriptural idea is by no means anti-Jewish in their eyes—the Jews can come too if they somehow manage to deny their God implanted heritage and become Gentiles! Then they also can be saved!

Of course, this might not be the worst guess in the world by theologians representing a humanity that is prone to error and looks to a God that forgives so that we can pick up and try again. But there are two problems. First, we're the ones who on stumbling give it another try, not our God. And second, unless one applies a "cut and paste" mentality to his Scriptural exegesis, this improbable absurdity is in no translation of the Bible I have yet seen!

A third Constantinian spawned error of judgment could even be misconstrued to be a genuine Abrahamic approach—except not the kind that the Almighty was impressed with! Remember when Abraham got itchy in waiting for God to give him his promised son and finally took matters into his own hands?[12] Whenever you take matters into your own hands, you are likely to inherit an *Ishmael* and the dubious rewards of this nature tend to not disappear all that quickly!

And so it was that a couple hundred years ago when the Bible scholars and devout theologians had a look around Jerusalem and old Judea—never mind that Emperor Hadrian had already renamed it *Falastina*—they surveyed all this holy dust and wretched rocks and duly surmised that not even the Almighty Himself could resurrect this place!

Classically, the celebrated Mark Twain—who was not all that much of a true believer himself—took a trip to the Holy Land where it once all happened and wrote in his chronicles that he had never seen such a God-forsaken place in his life. Descriptively he penned:

"Close to it was a stream, and on its banks a great herd of curious-looking Syrian goats and sheep were gratefully eating

---

12. Gen. 16; 21:1-21.

gravel. I do not state this as a petrified fact—I only suppose they were eating gravel, because there did not appear to be any thing else for them to eat."[13]

Twain also wrote:

"Come to Galilee....these unpeopled deserts, these rusty mounds of barrenness, that never, never, never do shake the glare from their harsh outlines....that melancholy ruin of Capernaum...we reached Tabor safely...we never saw a human being on the whole route.

"Bethlehem and Bethany in their poverty and their humiliation, have nothing about them now...the hallowed spot where the shepherds watched their flocks by night, and where the angels sang, 'Peace on earth, good will to men,' is untenanted by any living creature...Bethsaida and Chorazin have vanished from the earth, and the 'desert places' round about them sleep in the hush of a solitude that is inhabited only by birds of prey and skulking foxes.

"Stirring scenes...occur in the valley of Jezreel no more. There is not a solitary village throughout its whole extent—not for thirty miles in either direction. Palestine sits in sackcloth and ashes....desolate and unlovely...it is a dreamland."[14]

So the theologians of that day might well be forgiven to conclude, therefore, that when the Scriptures tantalize us some 800 times with the legacy that is Jerusalem, and when Isaiah and his fellow prophets spoke delectably of the glorious restoration of Jerusalem, well, they obviously must be talking about somewhere else! So they spiritualized that this new Jerusalem, to which we all aspire, must certainly have its setting in some other realm—say at least a little on the other side of planet Jupiter! They might be forgiven, that is, if their exegesis of the cosmology of the heavens

13. Mark Twain, *The Innocents Abroad*, (New York: Literary Classics of the United States, 1984).

14. Twain, *The Innocents Abroad*, 349, 441-442.

had been a wee bit more realistic, and forgiven if it is determined that sand, rocks, stars, and sky are legitimate substitutes for the Scriptures. I somehow opt for the Word of God.

It cannot be coincidence that the writings of 16 out of 17 of God's prophets in the *Tanakh* contain at least some small reflection toward the re-establishment of Israel in general and restoration of Jerusalem in particular.

Isaiah occupies nearly half his book to this very theme, and Zechariah and Ezekiel are not far behind. Other of the minor prophets like Nahum and Obadiah, whose prophecies are preoccupied with proclamation against God's foes, even contain a brief glimmer of hope of a new day for Judea and for Jerusalem.[15] Out of the entire 17 Old Testament prophets, only Jonah fails any mention of the restoration, but of course, no one would deny that there always was something a bit "fishy" about him!

But the fourth and final stigma of the discreditable emperor's anti-Semitic shadow over the Church, incredibly invades the very camp of those faithful who pride themselves most highly in a meticulous adherence to the Scriptures. Chapter and verse—we have had it all painstakingly laid out for decades on end that, by and large, it doesn't matter what happens to the Jews anyway—the really *righteous ones* won't be here to see it transpire. They will be gone to reside somewhere in the galaxies—the Bible never does quite clarify where—for a seven-year span while the rest of the world goes up in a puff of blue smoke. The concept is a half truth, and the context is twisted.

This theory—and it's barely a theory—has been popularized and paperbacked *ad nauseum* in certain segments of the Western world to the point where multitudes of the ought-to-be enlightened are irreparably hooked. Athough it is true that a handful of "key" Bible verses have been juggled and juxtaposed to support the much trumpeted theory, it is unfortunate that these texts have been ingeniously pulled from context and forced together like pieces of a jigsaw puzzle that almost seem to fit, but

---

15.   Obad. 17; Nah. 1:15.

then have to be forced a wee bit to "complete the picture." Sadly, in the end there are those few pieces leftover. No worries. Never let the facts get in the way of a good sermon!

But how could such sanctified Bible scholars ever stray so far off course? Of a certainty, Dr. C.I. Scofield was an accredited and acknowledged Bible scholar from the late nineteenth and early twentieth centuries. But a greater certainty is the well known word from Peter noting "that no prophecy of the Scripture is of any private interpretation."[16] I wish to subtly underline the principle that we all do make mistakes!

In Dr. Scofield's introduction to his *Scofield Reference Bible* he states,

> "It was felt that the old system of references, based solely upon the *accident* [italics mine] of the English words, was unscientific and often misleading. In the present edition, by a new system of connected topical references, all the greater truths of the divine revelation are so traced through the entire Bible from the place of first mention to the last that the reader may for himself follow the gradual unfolding of these, by many inspired writers through many ages, to their culmination in Jesus Christ and the New Testament Scriptures."[17]

He refers to the "old system" as an "*accident* of the English words" that was "unscientific and misleading". Presumably what he means by *accident* is that Greek and Hebrew roots do not always correspond to an exact English equivalent, which a good translator must, of course, accurately interpret for his readers. His preference, however, was to substitute a study system of related *topics* instead of those unscientific *words*.

Very interesting! In Chapter 5, we presented the "Two or Three Principle," which reinforces the Most High's pronouncements throughout Scripture by numerous repetitions of a unit word or phrase, or even

---

16. 2 Pet. 1:20 KJV.

17. Introduction, *Scofield Reference Bible*, iii, edited by Dr. C.I. Scofield, D.D., (New York: Oxford University Press, 1909).

an entire text. Word roots are not fluid like topics. In fact, roots reflect inseparable relationships. Moreover, we have demonstrated that the purpose of the Almighty is to drive home His message with repetition. And in this His Word uses *words*!

So to get a bit more *scientific*, Dr. Scofield instituted "a new system of topical references", giving us, it would appear, a substituted system of demoting the authentic *words* (or word roots) of Scripture to the advantage of ideas or interpretation of ideas. How did this one ever get past the fruit inspectors! It echoes of the antiquated child's game of "telephone" (some days before Nintendo) where a phrase was whispered into the first ear and passed down the line until the last child revealed the improbable distortion of the original. So follows the potential of the topical *idea*. Falling within the pale of an ever-so-subtle departure from the initial truth, once having moved off the initial root meaning, ensuing concepts can produce a disturbing variety of theological mutations. For our concerns, we shall soon see, it was the status of the Jew before his God. So much for *scientific* topical references. One *accident* gives rise to another!

Further on his Introduction, Scofield also impresses us with one of St. Augustine's maxims: "Distinguish the ages, and the Scriptures harmonize."[18] Except that the Infinite One may have always looked at things a bit differently than we impatient earthlings who are locked into time! To chop our Bibles into segments with a meat cleaver would be a horrific desecration. Dare I chop it with a pen?

For sure Augustine came up with much better stuff than that particular insight, but Dr. Scofield liked it, so here we are! We have neither time nor cause here to evaluate his dispensational theories except for one particular tangent of Dr. Scofield's postulations. The Jew ultimately got put into one box and the Gentile in another. The concept actually gives one a bit of a shiver in reminiscence of the "Old South" syndrome in the rampantly racist days of a "separate but equal" mentality in America.

It would appear, however, that the otherwise talented teacher did feel a few tugs of Christian remorse from the legacy of Constantine the

---

18.   Scofield, Introduction, *Scofield Reference Bible.*

Innovator; he began to notice—as many more of us are wont to do in these days—that our Jewish side of the Abrahamic family actually did have a reasonably high profile in the Scriptures. So in an effort to resolve the problem, and with the help of a dispensational Band-Aid or two, he came up with the idea that the Gentile Church would be saved first. Eventually the Jews would follow in their own turn—follow, that is, an additional seven year sentence of necessary—in less than sensitive Gentile eyes—chastisement. Both boxes will be neatly gift wrapped, as it were, for the Kingdom Age.

Now this would be a yawn, except for the fact that millions of well-meaning Christians in the Western world have swallowed this theory without batting an eye. Nor can you ever find this preposterous segregation in the Scriptures unless you hold a Scofield Bible that is significantly seasoned with the good doctor's notes. In fact, what you *will find* is the 180 degree opposite, as we have earlier on endeavored to clarify with a long march of texts from one end of Scripture to the other.

God forbid that we denigrate this servant of God's other noble efforts to enlighten the student of the Word, but this ignoble faux pas cannot be passed over without a just exposure. It is one more projectile from Connie's pet porcupine that is exceedingly distressful. Indeed, it does appear that there may even have been a mild recourse by the famous teacher to somehow counterbalance this latest quill of anti-Semitism. But this is not so. The tip remains embedded, and so does the pain.

If anyone has divine enlightenment that the Bible is built on something other than the historic interaction of the God of Abraham with his Jewish nation, climaxing in a covering of redemption for them as well as the whole world—a programming of salvation that finally ends with their new Jerusalem descending from Heaven with names of their 12 tribes inscribed on the gates, I must be wasting his time. We could well part company at this point. But if there is an inkling that May 14, 1948 and June 4, 1967[19]—two ineffaceable dates from our generation and our

---

19. The respective dates of the Declaration of Independence of the reborn State of Israel, and the return of the sacred Temple Mount with the entirety of Jerusalem back into the hands of her ancient people.

time—hold momentous prophetic relevance to our destiny and the destiny of the entire race, we do have much more to unfold quite over and above this tragic anti-Semitism that has spanned pharaohs and kings, emperors and tyrants, terrorists and even the well-meaning theologians.

Chapter 8

Is There Life After...Constantine?

We have just looked at several variations of anti-Semitic models that have been conjured up to falsify a Father God fed up with His first attempt at creating family, and who then it would be presumed, goes for a second try to get it right. But "God is not a man that He should lie, nor a son of man, that He should change His mind...."[1] For all scenarios that have been concocted to suggest that the Almighty has broken His promise to Abraham, by sheer contrast, there are even more models to demonstrate that not only is His covenant with His chosen seed forever in place, but also that those Gentiles who have come to adoption through His Son are very much an inseparable part of the whole plan.

From the letter to the Ephesians, we have already seen our first model. Paul unfolds a *mystery* in the hitherto unknown provision to also include the once-pagan Gentiles in God's redemption. Incorporated into His initial promise to Abraham, those nations—the *goyim*—had had little if any concept of a singular allegiance to the one and only El Shaddai and were therefore, "Excluded from citizenship in Israel and foreigners to the covenants of the promise...."[2] But these former outsiders were now

---

1. Num. 23:19a.

2. Eph. 2:12b.

in line for adoption into the Abrahamic family with full rights, entitlements and inheritance along with the original bloodline.[3] Coupled with Yeshua's several allusions to His "other sheep, that are not of this sheep pen,"[4] the Father's initial interest and purpose of one and one only family of promise is very clear. One family is for fellowship with the Father.

A second model is that of one and one only *Body.* Her name is figuratively called *Hephzibah,* and in Isaiah 62, she is to be married to the Lord. In a parallel reference, she is referred to as the *bride* of the Lamb in Revelation 21. She is featured in detail throughout Ephesians and various other of Paul's letters as the *Body of Messiah,* as we detailed in Chapter 5. New Testament teaching indelibly expresses that her body is indisputably composed of Jew and Gentile as one people in Christ. Paul writes to the Corinthians who were a part of that body that "I am jealous for you with a godly jealousy. I promised you to one husband, to Christ, so that I might present you as a pure virgin to Him."[5] And so we have one bride only—simultaneously modeled as the *Body*—for the Bridegroom.

A third model depicts joint heirs of one Promise, and a fourth presents a shared partnership in a one unique Covenant[6] with one eternal God. Both models are straightforward in Scripture and understood well enough that there is no need to further underscore either. They illustrate one divine promise for one people, and one Heaven-initiated contract to effect the unfathomable mercy of the Most High upon an equally shared destiny for both Jew and Gentile.

---

3.   Eph. 3:6.

4.   Jn. 10:16.

5.   2 Cor. 11:2.

6.   The expression of an Old and a New Covenant is hardly to be misconstrued as two separate covenants, or one covenant for one people with an alternative for the other. No Scripture whatsoever would even suggest this idea. The "new" aspect of the New Covenant is that God Himself takes the initiative to seal the relationship along with the New Testament provision of a new Lamb for the occasion. See Jeremiah 31:31-34, which is reiterated in Ezekiel 36:24-28. Though the return to the Land of Israel in the latter text applies primarily to the exiled half of the family, both expressions of God's mercy and restoration apply equally to Jew or Gentile.

Is There Life After...Constantine?

But now let us proceed on to have a look at one more fascinating model in the *Tanakh*. Since it is not featured in the New Testament, it may certainly be a less familiar illustration to many Gentile believers, if not an even more cryptic presentation of the Almighty's intended future bond between Jew and Gentile. In Chapter 37 of the prophecies of Ezekiel—just on the heels of the graphic imagery of the Valley of Dry Bones rustling, rattling, and rising to life as the resurrected "whole House of Israel"—the prophet presents the Lord's message in foretelling of the two sticks that become forever one.

God instructs Ezekiel to take two sticks and write on one "Of Judah and the Israelites associated with him" and on the other "Of Joseph—the stick of Ephraim—and all the House of Israel associated with him."[7]

He then tells Ezekiel to bring them together so that they become "one stick" in his hand, and He continues His allegory by instructing the prophet that when his countrymen question what all this means, he should inform them that this is what the Sovereign Lord says:

I am going to take the Israelite people from among the nations they have gone to, and gather them from every quarter and bring them to their own land. I will make them a single nation in the land, on the hills of Israel, and one king shall be king of them all. Never again shall they be two nations, and never again shall they be divided into two kingdoms. Nor shall they ever again defile themselves by their fetishes and their abhorrent things, and by their other transgressions. I will save them in all their settlements where they sinned, and I will cleanse them. Then they shall be My people, and I will be their God. My servant David shall be king over them; there shall be one shepherd for all of them. They shall follow My rules and faithfully obey My laws. Thus they shall remain in the land which I gave to My servant Jacob and in which your fathers dwelt; they and

---

7.   Ezek. 37:16, from *The TANAKH: The New JPS Translation According to the Traditional Hebrew Text*. Copyright 1985 by the Jewish Publication Society. Used by Permission.

their children and their children's children shall dwell there forever, with My servant David as their prince for all time. I will make a covenant of friendship with them—it shall be an everlasting covenant with them—I will establish them and multiply them, and I will place My Sanctuary among them forever. My Presence shall rest over them; I will be their God and they shall be My people. And when My Sanctuary abides among them forever, the nations shall know that I the LORD do sanctify Israel" (Ezekiel 37:21-28).[8]

Now, to the God-fearing Jew, the above portion is as transparent and beautiful as a crystal-clear stream, and despite a trend to godlessness and secularization from Tel Aviv to Miami Beach, there are still a fair number of the faithful waiting in the wings. In fact you'll find a good many of them solidly anchored among those "despicable settlers" dwelling on the so-called "West Bank" (read: land of Israel), not so subtly slandered by CNN, the BBC, and the entire gamut of a worldwide humanistic news media as the deplorable "enemies of peace." It becomes increasingly distressing to navigate a world that labels light as darkness while at the same time hailing violence the virtue. But the good news is that the above pledges of ultimate justice from the prophet Ezekiel will still be around long after CNN has gone off the air for the long night—notwithstanding that the current routine is a 24-hour broadcast!

But back to our text. A cursory glance might elicit the conclusion that it's an interesting bit of Bible that should arouse the Jews, but who knows when? Anyway, I'm not Jewish, and I'd rather get focused into my Gentile promises in Jesus. Of course yours are the very eyes that we would encourage to open a bit wider. Don't be too sure that Yeshua doesn't have His hand in this one too! It's very obvious from all we have said so far that this prophecy has also begun to fall into place in this century, and as the pace quickens into the new millennium, these ancient words of Ezekiel are correspondingly picking up momentum for our very generation.

---

8. Ezek. 37:21-28, from *The TANAKH: The New JPS Translation According to the Traditional Hebrew Text*. Copyright 1985 by the Jewish Publication Society. Used by Permission.

Is There Life After...Constantine?

So if it's an impressive promise for our Jewish family, it's imposing for me as well. If we've learned anything thus far in these pages: "What's good for the goose is good for the gander." May I restructure that one please: *"What's good for the Jews is good for me!"*

But on the other hand, how could I, as a *goy*, get involved with this all-Jewish scenario except to cheer from the bleachers? From the context it seems a bit far out to try to link this tribally structured "two-sticks-joined-forever-into-one" model with the other previous New Testament patterns of relationships. But is it really? Let's have a look at other Scriptures that lie behind it.

Identifying the stick "Belonging to Judah and the Israelites associated with him"[9] poses little problem. The Jews we know today are by and large from the Tribe of Judah, but not without a broad contingent of Benjamites who were a part of the Southern Kingdom as well. Also not to be overlooked were the Levites whose priestly service had been shared among the entire 12 tribes and who likewise had a significant representation among the descendants of Judah. And finally, it is a probability that a few scattered remnants among world Jewry today may even be descendent from all ten of the otherwise "lost" tribes, whose majority exile dated from the time of the Assyrian invasion in 722 B.C.[10]

So identifying "Judah and the Israelites associated with him" is clear cut. But "Ephriam's stick, belonging to Joseph and all the house of Israel associated with him" holds considerable more intrigue. Let's keep going.

---

9.   Ezek. 37:16.

10.   In Second Chronicles 30, it is recorded that a representation from all the ten tribes of Israel was present when early in his reign, King Hezekiah sent invitations throughout the land of Israel to come up to Jerusalem to celebrate the Passover. Historians differ whether this event may have taken place before or after the 722 B.C. exile of the ten tribes to Assyria. If it was after the exile, then there is no doubt that a representation of all the tribes, though most in very diminished numbers, constitute world Jewry today.

Where Is the Body?

Joseph, of course, was the cherished son of the Patriarch Jacob, and the great grandson of our family founder, Abraham. In the fallout of his father's scarcely veiled favoritism, Joseph was brutally sold into cruel bondage in Egypt by his bitterly jealous brothers. But after 13 years of demise in the dungeons of Egypt, his absolutely miraculous and meteoric rise to serve as prime minister to Pharaoh brought him into the world spotlight. Rediscovered by his family at the end of the era, he again became the prime adoration of his aging father, and due to the ignominious default of his frequently less-than-unblemished older brothers, he fell heir to the rights and privileges of the Jewish firstborn—the double blessing. As a result, instead of the traditional share of one twelfth of the inheritance, the highly exalted Joseph was honored the second portion over and above that received by his 11 brothers. In time-tested Jewish tradition, Joseph became the indirect recipient in that his two sons— Ephraim and Manasseh—were each awarded a full portion of the inheritance alongside that allotted to their 11 uncles.[11]

Thus, in future generations, Joseph the scepter of excellence in the household of his Father Jacob (whom God had some years previously renamed *Israel*) was represented by *both* his sons, Ephraim and Manasseh, as family successors to the Patriarchs. Moreover, Ephraim, like his father, though not the traditionally designated eldest son, received the birthright anyway by the deliberate choice of Grandfather Jacob.[12] In generations to come, after the death of Solomon and the nation of Israel became divided into two, the Southern Kingdom, representing the tribes of Judah and Benjamin, became known as the Kingdom of Judah while the remaining ten tribes comprising the Northern Kingdom were regarded as the Kingdom of Israel. And it was neither by default nor accident of history that they were synonymously referred to as Ephraim, the younger son of the beloved Joseph.

And so it is that our text in Ezekiel 37 speaks of a stick "Belonging to Judah and the Israelites associated with him," and another stick, "Ephraim's stick, belonging to Joseph and all the house of Israel associated with him."

---

11. The entire moving account is a classic in any literary league and is found in Genesis 37–49.

12. Gen. 48:17-22.

Is There Life After...Constantine?

But that was ancient prophecy from ancient times. What can we make of it today? Well, it just so happens that after nearly 2,000 years, the latter-day descendants of Judah—and those that a kaleidoscopic tumble of Scripture, history, geography, and destiny have allied with him—are clearly back in the land in these seeming "end of days." They began as a trickle at the end of the nineteenth century, grew to a flowing stream in the first half of the twentieth and finally became a deluge in 1948 and the years that followed.

That's nice. But whatever happened to highly esteemed Joseph, overcomer, hero, and beloved of his father? Joseph was cast into a role played out by son Ephraim, who these days unfortunately holds more of a stigma of his uncles that were *lost* into oblivion than that of his famous father who was ultimately found alive and well in Egypt. It just doesn't seem to square up that Joseph—who was short-listed in the Scriptures (very short, I might add) as one with whom no sin was ever associated—should end up as the less than flattering Patriarchal totem of "the ten lost tribes"?

Well, many a theory has sprung up about what might have happened to those "lost tribes." Spurious cults, whose credibility is somewhat distanced from reality, have attempted to make mileage from the unresolved disappearance, while slightly more plausible claims have been registered from Scandinavia to China.[13] Candidacy for the honors have also surfaced in India, among the Karen tribespeople in northeastern Burma and even in the remote Southern Highlands of Papua New Guinea.[14]

---

13. The author had a friend at university who was a Chinese Jew, which is not at all an unheard of ethnic combination, though most would put the origin of that lineage into much more recent times. Likewise, an interesting theory of links in Scandinavia has been published in two articles in *Jezreel's Call* (Lenoir, NC, USA), "Will the Lost Tribes Return?" Dennis Jones, April 1995, and "Were the Lost Tribes Ever Really Lost?" James Tabor, December 1995

14. The author has also had personal contact with those Karens making the claim. This is hardly to lend legitimacy to the sources or accuracy of their legends, but to report that such assertions are widespread. The most fascinating data came in parallel reports of ancient Semitic linkage from two neighboring tribes in Papua New Guinea, published by the author in the *PNG Post Courier*, "Where Did We Come From," August 1992.

Where Is the Body?

On one hand, any starry-eyed admirer of Abraham could potentially come up with an adjusted ethnologue to make a good story. But from
another perspective, except for fascination and intrigue, does it really
matter? Perhaps it does. At least it does from the Ancient of Days' point
of view. He has been a precision planner. His accounting of detail is unri-
valed. And His precise predictions of that to come has been His signa-
ture: "Then they will know that I am the Lord!"[15]

In this same vein of investigation of genetic secrets that have been
locked up for aeons, recent DNA testing *has* yielded up some eye-popping
performance that relates to a *bona fide* identity of the *Kohanim* from the
tribe of Levi—the ancient inheritors of the Levitical priesthood.[16]

But aside from Papua New Guinea, DNA, and the occasion of Chinese Jews, is there perhaps another quite different level of information
according to the Almighty's manner of speaking sense to us? Indeed!
There are two challenging prophecies in the patriarchal blessings pro-
nounced by Israel near the end of his days. The first one was upon his
grandson Ephraim:

*Nevertheless, [Manasseh's] younger brother [Ephraim] will be
greater than he, and his descendants will become a **group of
nations** (Genesis 48:19b).*

The second one was included in Israel's final blessing upon his 12
sons. Just prior to his death he told them to "Gather around so I can tell
you what will happen to you in days to come."[17] When he came to Joseph,
his beloved, his pride and his joy, he prophesied:

*Joseph is a fruitful vine, a fruitful vine near a spring, whose
branches climb over a wall (Genesis 49:22).*

The former text says precisely what it says; the latter necessitates a
little more insight and evaluation. But scrutinize we will, and evaluate we

---

15. Ezek. 36:38, with over 20 identical references elsewhere in Ezekiel.

16. "Genetic Link Found Among Kohanim," *Jerusalem Post*, January 3, 1997.

17. Gen. 49:1.

must! *A vine running over a wall* does strongly suggest a reaching out, a spreading out, and a growing away from one's original boundaries. This is precisely the scenario that Joseph was called upon to enter when he was cast out as a slave into Egypt, far away from his former roots. And it was far from those roots that he grew and he prospered until he ultimately came into his own.

But Israel's final patriarchal blessing upon Joseph was a prophecy, not a history! Was he speaking over his cherished son that in his succeeding generations history would in some manner repeat itself?

If this were the only text, any such projected interpretation could be extremely shaky, particularly so when considering our "Two or Three Principle" that Scripture requires to underscore accuracy. But the above two prophetic references taken together certainly do suggest Ephraim will ultimately be projected to *extra-national* and *extra-geographical* dimensions.

And finally, there is one more unique verse from the prophecy of Zechariah that realistically bears some thought-provoking connections:

> *This is what the Lord Almighty says, "In those days ten men from all languages and nations will take firm hold of one Jew by the hem of his robe and say, "Let us go with you, because we have heard that God is with you"* (Zechariah 8:23).

As we have already noted, with the exception of a straggling few who remained, there were ten tribes that were scattered to Assyria and beyond in 722 B.C. With little or no precise historical records to follow them, these were eventually lost from the ledger.

But back to our primary text in Ezekiel, the Lord has emphatically prophesied that He will ultimately reunite Ephraim—His designation for those ten tribes that have seemingly evaporated from history—with Judah as "stick to stick," *never again* to be broken apart. So does the Almighty yet have some profound genetic surprises tucked away for us just around the corner?

Where Is the Body?

Or could it even be that the Most High will put this one into the "too hard" basket, that it will never happen, just like some used to say that it would be impossible for the Jews to ever come back home to their promised land? (Ironically, some of these same doubting Thomases are now saying out of the other side of their mouths that the land doesn't belong to the Jews anyway!)

But there's one more option. Perhaps He yet has some other cryptic twist to fulfill this one before our very eyes, something that will truly amaze us.

Have we adopted Gentiles grown so tall in our perceived spirituality, so staid in our doctrines, so smug in our status that we have drifted far, far away from the conscious presence of an awesome God that is a stickler for precision? I can assure you, when it comes to His promises—and that includes His prophecies—He'll not miss a beat!

As we detailed in Chapter 7, there is a still a disturbing amount of ignorance and anti-Semitism among much of the Christian Church to this very day. Nevertheless, there is also within almost every denominational boundary, a small but solid percentage of Gentile believers who love, respect, and even sense an unexplainable inner relationship with their Jewish brethren. This phenomenon is much more prevalent in the Third World than in the "enlightened" West.

The awareness that the Bible belongs to the Jews, and the Jews belong to the Bible, is almost universal among the strongly Christian countries throughout the Pacific Islands where we have spent the majority of our lives and ministry. A sheer awe and respect for the Jew is present even among those Third World congregations that ironically sprang from very anti-Semitic Church backgrounds in the sending countries. I am most familiar with the Pacific Islands. But this is also true in Africa. It is true in Brazil. It is true among Christians in Asia. Except for the cults that have their own agenda, it is true in almost every major Third World country across the Christian spectrum. Perhaps it always has been this way, going all the way back to the beginning of the original Gentiles, impressed by and looking to a Jewish Messiah.

Is There Life After...Constantine?

Only the West got their wires crossed by Constantine & Company. Spreading throughout Europe, across to the New World in North America and all the way down to Australia and New Zealand, "superior" knowledge and a bit of ethnic pride completed the short circuit. But even then, there's that minority in the West as well that can't explain why they feel the way they do for the rest of their estranged and long lost Jewish family.

So with our two prophetic sticks in one hand and a clear mirror in the other, let's take a sober look at this one more model that the Lord Almighty has to show us.

Ten tribes have been sadly "lost." They were Abraham's family; they were God's family, but because of idolatry, they were mercilessly dragged off. They're gone! But again there are those from across every Christian persuasion *from every nation* who have spontaneously grasped the robe of Jesus the Jew, and in doing so unwittingly elected to fill in the depleted ranks from those ten "lost tribes" now swallowed into oblivion across the globe. Thus each nation compassing the earth may in a figure, ultimately present to Him who sits upon the Throne, her sons who have been born into the Family of Abraham through the blood of Yeshua. He could even divide them as it were into ten groups, each established into ten ranks to replace the fallen from ten tribes. In review, we see that Zechariah has finalized the prophecy:

This is what the Lord Almighty says: "In those days ten men from all languages and nations will take firm hold of one Jew by the hem of his robe and say, 'Let us go with you, because we have heard that God is with you'" (Zechariah 8:23).

And the Sovereign Lord has promised to join the sticks:

...I am going to take the stick of Joseph—which is in Ephraim's hand—and of the Israelite tribes associated with him, and join it to Judah's stick, making them a single stick of wood, and they will become one in My hand (Ezekiel 37:19).

And that the Sovereign Lord continues to complete His end of days parable:

...Never again shall they be two nations, and never again shall they be divided into two kingdoms...My servant David shall be king over them; there shall be one shepherd for all of them. They shall follow My rules and faithfully obey My laws...and I will place My Sanctuary among them forever. My Presence shall rest over them; I will be their God and they shall be My people. And when My Sanctuary abides among them forever, the nations shall know that I the LORD do sanctify Israel (Ezekiel 37:22-28).[18]

If the two sticks of Ezekiel 37 were but some isolated guesswork to conjure up an interesting parable postulating eventual Jew and Gentile interparticipation, it would be flimsy indeed. But taken together in a lengthening chain along with all the other models, the repetition of types is continually reinforced. And the irrefutable accuracy of the Almighty's ultimate intention expands into an ever-broadening base. Nor is this the last of the endless models of Jewish-Gentile interrelationship with which the God of the Bible has permeated His Scriptures. There are more to come.

We should break off this chapter at this point, but something deep within forbids me to leave the sensational and heart-rending story of Joseph without a reference to—in my opinion—the most graphic of all the types of Yeshua the Messiah in the whole of Scripture. Up to now we have presented five models of inseparability of the family of Abraham, one of which the Scriptures depict as the Bride of Christ. But I dare not leave the Genesis account of Joseph behind without one corresponding classic type of the Bridegroom. It is embodied in Joseph himself.[19]

He is at the first rejected by his own brothers. The motive was jealousy! By divine commission he is then alternately sent to save the Gentiles. In a remarkable parallel he begins His monumental task at 30 years of age. Once the Gentiles have been rescued, he in turn embraces his long-alienated family without a trace of resentment or recrimination. And

---

18. From *The TANAKH: The New JPS Translation According to the Traditional Hebrew Text.* Copyright 1985 by the Jewish Publication Society. Used by Permission.

19. Gen. 37–50.

Is There Life After...Constantine?

Pharaoh, the primary Gentile who has been spared of disaster, is delighted with it all. The once shadowy family of Joseph turns out to be the chosen people of Israel, who now move to front and center stage. There is no jealousy anymore, and so is it to be!

May we note, however, that envy and arrogance only returned when: "Now there arose up a new King over Egypt, which knew not Joseph."[20] Will a word to the wise be sufficient?

Our sixth model of scripturally decreed Jew and Gentile interdependence is the most graphically presented and most undeniable of all. In Romans Chapter 11, Paul characterizes the Gentile believers as *wild olive branches* grafted into the *original root* of the *cultivated olive tree*— that is, into the nation of Israel—rooted from the beginning into the Lord's promises to Abraham and his offspring.

> *If some of the branches have been broken off, and you, though a wild olive shoot, have been grafted in among the others and now share in the nourishing sap from the olive root, do not boast over those branches. If you do, consider this: You do not support the root, but the root supports you* (Romans 11:17-18).

Moreover, Paul adequately warns against any potential arrogance by those Gentile believers prone to condescension toward the natural family. It may come as a great shock to some, but evaluation of the performance of the Jewish branches has never been assigned to the Gentile members!

> *You will say then, "Branches were broken off so that I could be grafted in." Granted but they were broken off because of unbelief, and you stand by faith. Do not be arrogant, but be afraid. For if God did not spare the natural branches, he will not spare you either* (Romans 11:19-21).

Indeed, the family tree of Abraham, quite specifically turns out to be an olive tree! But this model is of such major consequence that we will consider it in its entirety in the next chapter.

---

20. Ex. 1:8, KJV.

Chapter 9

Two Olive Trees

God initially characterizes Israel, His people of promise, as an olive tree in the book of Jeremiah where the prophet declares the Lord's message:

The Lord called you a thriving olive tree with fruit beautiful in form... (Jeremiah 11:16).

This introduces a metaphor that winds through the Bible. Following our principle of God's repetition of a significant point that He chooses to underline, if we course through the Scriptures, not one but *two olive trees*—now and again expressed as "branches"—are mentioned together a further three times. The first is in Zechariah 4, the second is in the eleventh chapter of Paul's letter to the Romans, and finally once more in Revelation 11. We will begin chronologically with chapter 4 of Zechariah's book of prophecy.

Zerubbabel, then governor of Judah under the auspices of Babylon, had been nominated by God to begin in Jerusalem to head up a rebuilding of the beloved temple, which had been destroyed some 70 years earlier by the army of King Nebuchadnezzar. We might well conclude that in surveying the mountain of rocks, rubble, and ruin, poor old Zerubbabel was so overwhelmed by the enormity of the task that he required a bit of a boost from Above just to keep going. So it was that the Lord sent an angel to Zechariah with that classic message of encouragement for the faint-hearted in general and for Zerubbabel in particular:

"Not by might nor by power, but by My Spirit," says the Lord Almighty (Zechariah 4:6b).

But to drive the message home with a visual aid or two, the angel first had to arouse Zechariah out of a deep sleep, and then he showed him a vision of a solid gold lampstand with *two olive trees*, one to the right of the lampstand and the other one on the left. He asked if Zechariah understood the meaning of this awesome vision. When the prophet replied in the negative, the angel gave him the straightforward directive as in the text above: "It's not by might and it's not by power, but by My Spirit...."

That side of the communication seemed to come clear to Zechariah, and we can pretty well be assured that Zerubbabel got the message on time and must have been not a little motivated by it. But if we have a look at the end of Chapter 4, after it was all over the prophet still had a few questions about the whole affair: "Excuse me, sir Angel, but what do these two olive trees have to do with it anyway?" The text suggests that the angel seems to presume that Zechariah ought to have caught the basic significance by that time, so he randomly responds that:

...These are the two who are anointed to serve the Lord of all the earth (Zechariah 4:14).

And that was that! Now most of us might well sympathize with Zechariah. After all, he had been sleeping a mite soundly, and the angel had hardly been overly generous with his clues. But never mind, unlike Zechariah who came into the vision a bit cold, we have already taken our cue in the closing lines of our previous chapter, and it seems that all the rest of the world will just have to wait a few centuries until the great apostle finally issues a clear cut explanation in the Book of Romans.

And, of course, Romans did eventually get written with divine Pauline insights for an Abrahamic trust relationship for both Jew and

Two Olive Trees

Gentile with their God. In chapter 11 of that book, along with other irreversible plans for the redemption of the Jewish nation, Paul elucidates with graphic symbolism the meaning behind that metaphor of the two olive trees. In this case he speaks of the two sets of branches that symbolically bond the Jew and the Gentile believer together into an indivisible root.[1]

True to Jeremiah 11:16, Israel is God's primary Olive Tree, which He has cultivated from the time of Abraham. But through the scourge of disobedience over the ages, a number of its beautiful branches have been broken off through God's judgment. Now He introduces a *second* olive tree, a wild one from the bush, which represents the Gentile believers in Yeshua. In this trust relationship with the one and only God of the Universe, they have the unique privilege to be graciously grafted into the original root—not to be hovering above the other branches, nor to be situated below—but simply to be bonded into one and the same tree.

So to lengthen the growing list of our previous models of interrelationship, the two olive trees now yield to us one more replica of God the Father drawing Jew and Gentile together into one promise, one covenant, one Body, one Family, one unbreakable rod, and now *two distinct branches into one Olive Tree* of unmistakable significance. It is of essence that we note that the Gentile believers replace only *some* of the broken-off branches. It is not only ludicrous, but indicates a total ignorance of the Scriptures to suggest that the entire tree has now been replaced by the Gentile Church, as numerous anti-Semitic and consequently unenlightened theologians have concocted over the last several centuries.

So finally, we can appreciate clearly what the prophet Zechariah could not immediately grasp. That is, that the *two olive trees*, one on either side of the golden lampstand, represent both the Jewish and Gentile branches of the family of Abraham, both sides of the promised covenant of redemption, bonded and growing together, or at least it was so designed—as an eternally living entity.

---

1. Rom. 11:16-24.

Where Is the Body?

So why did the angel not give Zechariah a bit more information? Perhaps he did in a cryptic sort of way. Let's have a closer look. How many distinct parts did Zechariah see? He saw first *one* golden lampstand plus *two* olive trees, or a total of *three* items. And that happens to be the exact number of terms—three—that the angel used in his roundabout reply: *might*, *power*, and the *Spirit of God.*

Zerubbabel got the message clearly enough that human might and human power were not enough—in fact the permeation of that truth was what was so depressing in the first place. That mountain of rubble-come-responsibility could never, ever be moved without help from somewhere. But now with that message from the angel via Zechariah, the good governor could rise up in his spirit with the assurance that by the intervention of the *Ruach Ha Kodesh*, the Spirit of Almighty God, divine help was already on the way.

But as we relate this incident to a far more distant scope of this very same prophecy, we have no other message for the then far-in-the-future immovable mountains of our own day. Whether by Jewish intellectual might or by *goyim* spiritual power, there will *be no other way* to carry on except by the totally overriding intervention of the Spirit of the Almighty. That is the exact message that Israel needs to appropriate today as she seeks to remain afloat in a sea of seething Islamic hatred, which is driven by the gales of a godless and manipulative media. No less is the personal directive plus the dynamic power of the Holy Spirit the crying need of the Gentile believers at the jarring juncture of what we know as the twenty-first century!

A verse that ought to be an indelible text of Christian consciousness is Ephesians 2:8-9:

> *For it is by grace you have been saved, through faith—and this is not from yourselves, it is the gift of God—not by works, so that no one can boast* (Ephesians 2:8-9).

Yet, why is it that we consistently need to be reminded that it is exclusively by grace that we are saved? Moreover, it may well be an astonishing revelation to some learned churchmen that the Jewish successors of

Abraham have been promised eventual redemption by the identically same grace.[2]

It is "not of works, but a gift of God" just in case either side of the olive tree should like to pull rank on another of his fellow branches. Paul goes out of his way to emphasize this very forewarning to effect a mutual, non-arrogant relationship from one side of the metaphorical tree to the other.

Moreover, he spells out clearly that which puzzled the prophet, and quite rightly so. How was Zechariah to know that an initial rejection of the Messiah by His people would result in the execution of God's hidden agenda to eventually add the Gentiles into the family of Abraham, as we have already seen in the bombshell of the "mystery" spelled out in Ephesians? Paul even further drives the point home in Romans 11:

Again I ask: Did they stumble so as to fall beyond recovery? Not at all! Rather, because of their transgression, salvation has come to the Gentiles to make Israel envious. But if their transgression means riches for the world, and their loss means riches for the Gentiles, how much greater riches will their fullness bring! ... For if their rejection is the reconciliation of the world, what will their acceptance be but life from the dead? (Romans 11:11-12,15).

So at this point we have the relevance of the two olive trees in Zechariah 4 and now a more detailed elaboration in Romans 11. This brings us to our third and final occurrence of a prophetic reference to the *two olive trees* in a time frame much closer at hand. Give or take a few years—some may be generous with a decade—we are of a certainty far more contemporary with the events currently on the horizon of the Apocalypse, commonly known to many Bible readers as John the apostle's visions in the Book of Revelation. Let us hone in specifically on Revelation chapter 11.

---

2.   A comparative study of Ezekiel 36:24-27, as well as the whole of Zechariah 3, will be presented in Chapter 11. One could be forgiven for pondering if, at that glorious point of time, the recipients will even be asked if they desire the transformation!

Where Is the Body?

John was told in his vision that God would grant power to His two witnesses to prophesy for 1,260 days.[3] This enumeration also turns out to be precisely 42 months, three and a half years, or a time, times, and half a time—which can also be seen to be a pseudonym for three and a half years—all variations of which feature prominently in Revelation 11, 12, and 13 and serve as excellent rocket fuel for many an end time calculation. Nor should we be taken aback if the vision's figurative language might even in some way parallel or coincide with an added reference to *three and a half days* further on in the same chapter.[4]

Now these and similar numerical predictions, particularly from the prophecies of Daniel, have provided a field day for those Bible scholars quite skilled in the finer features of a little Bible game known as "Date Setters' Roulette." Unfortunately deadlines come and go, while advents and raptures are continually being revised, reprogrammed, and rescheduled. Of course, no one really ever wins the game, though there appears to be an abundance of losers, who rarely seem to rise from the ashes of their misfortune to collect their booby prizes.[5]

One problem just could be that all these intriguing numbers obviously do have real meaning, but rather than having a linear fulfillment, they are multi-dimensional. That is, they will have a repeat fulfillment at various levels of significance and at different stages of history, making them very difficult to pin down on any one chart.

This concept also brings to mind that for millennia man measured all his castles in three dimensions until earlier this century when Albert Einstein proposed that time must be reckoned as a fourth dimension. That insight could well drop a monkey wrench into the mathematics of the paperback prophets, along with a few adjustment factors that the King of

---

3. Rev. 11:3.

4. Rev. 11:11.

5. One fascinating exception from the run of routine theories that have largely been recycled and reiterated can be found in an intriguing work by Marvin Byers, *The Final Victory: The Year 2000* (Shippensburg: Destiny Image, 1994).

the universe may have decided not to disclose just yet.[6] Moreover a *fifth* dimension, which could feature the metaphysical is under discussion,[7] notwithstanding quantum physicists are currently pondering a total of nine dimensions! Need we emphasize that the prophetic enigmas of the Eternal Mind have long been oversimplified by those who don't have a clue what's going on? Surely, the One who told His disciples, "No one knows about that day or hour, not even the angels in heaven, nor the Son, but only the Father,"[8] quite certainly knew what He was talking about. He said what He meant and meant what He said.

So we must conclude that for beginners we had best dispense with that myriad of dates and days and years and times and simply focus on those *two witnesses*. A quite popular interpretation in a number of elite circles is that these two must be none other than Moses and Elijah who they have booked to return in something more than impressive fashion for what traditional Bible scholars render "the first half of Daniel's 70th week," that is, the presumed last seven years before the return of Messiah. More counting on fingers and toes!

But is it realistic to assume that these two witnesses are in fact two men and that their prophetic witness is indeed powerful messages to stir the fainthearted or even shake the nations? Does the Bible actually tell us that? Or is this merely a disingenuous guess inferred from our current day interpretation of a witness? Note that John immediately clarifies their identity—if not function—by declaring them to be God's *two olive trees*. Now our first two parallel texts afford us a very clear identification of what two olive trees represent in Scripture, not to mention the opening analogy of Jeremiah 11:16. God has symbolized the two halves of Abraham's family of promise as the two branches of *His Olive Tree*, and it

---

6. For an impressive biblical perspective on Einstein's work as it relates to time outside our terrestrial environment see "In the Beginning" by Gerald Schroeder, *Jerusalem Post International Edition*, Aug. 29, 1998 or his complete book, *Genesis and the Big Bang* (New York: Bantam Doubleday, 1992).

7. Michael Drosnin, *The Bible Code* (Great Britain: Simon & Schuster, 1997), 50, 196.

8. Mt. 24:36.

would be most extraordinary if that same identity did not continue on into Revelation. Again we must maintain our orientation with accuracy grounded on the basic premise of repetition of key terminology throughout Scripture.

But should there still be any lingering misgivings that we are not talking about a *bona fide* Moses and Elijah reappearing, perhaps we had better check our reasons for resistance. One might be that well-worn theories die hard—especially if they have someone's super spiritual stamp on them. Perhaps we could coin a phrase: "Old theological ideas never die, they just keep getting quoted!"

But for the best insight of all, it is paramount that we look again at the text. Let's finish the verse. The angel goes on to declare as a "second opinion" on who these two really might be. These are the two lampstands that stand before the Lord of the earth.[9] When lampstands are clearly labeled in chapter 1 of Revelation as churches or bodies of people, it takes a fair stretch of the imagination to hark back to the assumption that John is being informed of two—and only two—mortals who have re-entered history for a new assignment. As renowned as Moses and Elijah are—and they do unambiguously reflect a symbolic imagery of Israel and the Holy Spirit Age respectively—they do not begin to embody the entire glory of the total nation of Israel or the immense prestige of the entirety of the redeemed saints from among the Gentiles, those two immortal bodies that "stand before the Lord of the earth."

Western mentality almost automatically conjures up that a "witness" so described must be a powerful preacher with capacity of persuasion to strike awe at the most horrific of resistance. The real fact is that the most unremovable footprint, the most indelible mark and the greatest witness God has ever stamped before mankind has been the indestructibility of the Jew!

As detailed in earlier chapters—from Pharaoh to Arafat and from Haman to Hitler and Hamas—all manner of tyrants, dictators, kings, and terrorists have tried to rid the globe of the menace of the despised Jew but

---

9.   Rev. 11:4.

have miserably failed. Their tormentors from ages on end have been long destroyed in total ignominy, but God's chosen family still lives on.

Again, the celebrated Mark Twain, who in standard theological thinking was anything but a sanctioned spokesman for the Source of the Universe, pondered of the Jew:

"The Jews constitute but one percent of the human race...Properly the Jew ought hardly to be heard of; but he is heard of, has always been heard of. He is as prominent on the planet as any other people...He has made a marvelous fight in this world, in all the ages; and he has done it with his hands tied behind him...The Egyptian, the Babylonian, and the Persian rose, filled the planet with sound and splendor, then faded to dream-stuff and passed away; the Greek and the Roman followed, and made a vast noise, and they are gone; other peoples have sprung up and held their torch high for a time, but it burned out, and they sit in twilight now, or have vanished. The Jew saw them all, beat them all, and is now what he always was...All things are mortal but the Jew; all other forces pass, but he remains. What is the secret of his immortality?"[10]

But the exact parallel dynamic of indestructibility in the New Testament is Yeshua's declaration of the eternal destiny of the believing Gentile:

...upon this rock I will build My church, and the gates of hell shall not prevail against it (Matthew 16:18 KJV).

Along with the immortal Jew, the *gates of hell* neither have nor ever will be able to overthrow the Church, which through our Lord Jesus has been adopted into that imperishable family of promise, the family of Abraham.

---

10.   Mark Twain, *The Complete Essays of Mark Twain*, Charles Neider, ed. (New York: Doubleday, 1963), 249, as quoted in Netanyahu, *A Place Among the Nations* (New York: Bantam, 1993), 400.

Where Is the Body?

Nor has the olive tree been chosen at random from a forest of options without Divine intention. There stands an ancient olive tree in Gethsemane, just outside the Old City of Jerusalem, whose age is estimated to be somewhere between 2,000 to 3,000 years old. Yeshua might well have knelt under this one as well, and the *two huge branches* of this aged monarch awesomely remind today's more sensitive visitors to the garden of Paul's momentous symbolism of the renowned *Olive Tree* of Romans 11. Over the centuries branches have been broken off, while others issuing from the imperishable root have shot up in their stead. And the old legend remains. The *olive* is a tree that *never dies!*

Thus, the inherent hope of both Jew and Gentile will continue to live on until the Father's plan of the ages is forever fulfilled with a destiny of justice and righteousness for those redeemed from among His entire creation. I delight in how J.B. Phillips expressed Romans 8:18-19 in his translation:

> *In my opinion whatever we may have to go through now is less than nothing compared with the magnificent future God has planned for us. The whole creation is on tiptoe to see the wonderful sight of the sons of God coming into their own.*[11]

So let us momentarily step back in an overview of this section of the Apocalypse. After a string of nine other parallel references throughout the entirety of New Testament, we need to take special notice that God's boast of the eternal destiny of His two witnesses in Revelation 11, follows almost directly on the heels of the tenth and final mention of our earlier unveiled "mystery":

> *But in the days when the seventh angel is about to sound his trumpet, the mystery of God will be accomplished, just as he announced to his servants the prophets* (Revelation 10:7).

This announcement of the final fulfillment of the "mystery of God"—the inclusion of the Gentiles into the promised inheritance of Abraham—is then immediately followed in chapter 11 with the Ancient

---

11.   J.B. Phillips, *The New Testament in Modern English* (London: Macmillan, 1965).

of Days' exhibition to the universe of His proud achievement in the inde-structible double witness of His two olive trees, His two candlesticks, His twofold light, His imperishable family of Jew and Gentile blended into one and one only *Body*.

And directly following this allegory of our two witnesses, comes the blast of the celebrated seventh trumpet[12] with the climactic universal proclamation of the now worldwide echo of Handel's Messiah:

> *Then the seventh angel blew his trumpet, and there were loud voices in heaven, saying: "The kingdom of the world has become the kingdom of our Lord and of His Messiah, and He will reign forever and ever"* (Revelation 11:15 NRS).

But we have not yet finished with our focus on our two witnesses. Let's go back. If one represents Israel and the other the adopted Gentile Church, what might we make of all those miracles in the "days of their prophesying"? For a start, it has all happened *at least once* long ago. It is a recognized fact that prophecy may be fulfilled more than once in ever increasing significance, much like the ever expanding rings emanating out from the pebble tossed into a pond. Whether we will see a repeat cycle or even part of a cycle is quite irrelevant. Thus, reflecting on the actual miracles of the original Moses and the real Elijah from back in their day, Israel the witness has already "been there" and "done that" for all the world to see.

And what about those fascinating numbers spelling out the duration of the various sequences? Now we can count off 1,260 days—or are they years? Or both? It doesn't take too much mathematical insight beyond the art of counting fingers and toes to decide that three and a half years describes the same time span, as does 42 months. Or does it? You can put your shoes and socks back on now. The longer dimension may be God's cryptic way to span centuries while the shorter dare compress a breath.

Another quite variant insight that I gleaned from my "University of Stone Age Technology," three and a half in a non-technical society

---

12.   1 Cor. 15:51-52; 1 Thess. 4:16; Mt. 24:31.

generally may mean little more than halfway to seven, the classic biblical number of *completion*. Moreover, we will do well to note that in original Eastern description, "half" need not always be a precise 50 percent! The perceptive will be aware that the Bible was inscribed in the matrix of a spiritually sensitive East, and hardly in the technically tethered Western world.

Of course those numbers are there for a reason. But that reason does not happen to be for polishing crystal balls! Furthermore, they will afford limited assistance as we focus primarily on our fundamental search for a sometimes elusive *Body*. Suffice it to say that in the eternal witness of God's two powerful anointed ones that spans the ages, He has left on the earth the indestructible footprints of His quite imperishable *two olive trees*.

One thing we may know with certainty, His timing will be perfect and His mathematics precise. Prophecy was neither given for purposes of personal publicity, nor for profiteering on publications of how and when it will all come off. We are warned only to be ready. But of course when all does unfold, we will look back with not a little awe as we reflect upon His own incredible precision, His ingenuity and His unique timing. The real purpose of prophecy will be sensed in His oft-repeated proclamation through His prophets:

> ...*Then they will know that I am the Lord* (Ezekiel 36:38).

But now we must hasten on to the final scene of this whole allegory. And indeed, this closing scenario gets to be a bit gruesome. It makes you see why the majority of the Church—theologians included—have voted in this era of human rights and democratic privilege to let Moses and Elijah come back to take care of this whole messy business, while Gentile believers fly off on a seven-year holiday somewhere beyond the blue. A three and a half year sabbatical might even serve the purpose!

Back to our text. We learn that the vicious beast of end-times notoriety attacks those two witnesses and actually kills them. What on earth is happening with their invincibility? Here's how the vision goes:

94

Two Olive Trees

Now when [the two witnesses] *have finished their testimony, the beast that comes up from the Abyss will attack them, and overpower and kill them. Their bodies will lie in the street of the great city, which is figuratively called Sodom and Egypt, where also their Lord was crucified. For three and a half days men from every people, tribe, language and nation will gaze on their bodies and refuse them burial. The inhabitants of the earth will gloat over them and will celebrate by sending each other gifts, because these two prophets had tormented those who live on the earth* (Revelation 11:7-10).

He chops down God's *two olive trees*, as it were, and their dead bodies lie in the street for—in "cousin" numerology suggesting a much shorter metaphor—three and a half days. We recall that the vision started by relating to years, but here we have an abrupt shift to days. For one thing it does not make a realistic analogy for dead bodies to lie in a street without burial for three and a half years. For another, the Ancient of Days is not in the habit of passing out last days calendars. So calculators are out and Holy Spirit sensitivity to the times is in. And if I remember properly, this is all Yeshua told us do in the first place:

Therefore keep watch, because you do not know on what day your Lord will come (Matthew 24:42).

But unfortunately the seven-year-come-three-and-a-half-year mentality has left such a deep Goodyear tread upon the brains of some of us, it is imperative that I warn you again that God's final countdown may hardly be as symmetrical as the opening verses of Revelation would tantalize the naïve to presume. Moreover, should the more brilliant among my readers throw my caution to the winds, coming up with a perfect calculation, I have one more verse for you:

...but for the sake of the elect those days will be shortened (Matthew 24:22).

So your figures are still wrong. The family gets a discount, and it might be a pretty nice one at that!

95

Where Is the Body?

Nevertheless, it is quite clear that the beast most terrible will be out to destroy not one but *both* of the Almighty's olive trees in His final burst of wrath. So what else is new? We should recall that some of the key architects of the New Age movement declared long ago that the only hope to eventually come up with a decent world will be to eliminate the *Judeo-Christian tradition.*[13] That these deliberately godless designs of the day are strategically directed against *both branches* of the Olive Tree, should serve to jolt the less alert among the Gentile believers to the accuracy of Yeshua's pronouncement that "the children of this world...are wiser than the children of light."[14]

But now we come to the uncomfortable part. Who wants to be a dead body lying in the street anyway—even for three and a half days? The whole concept is very disturbing, collectively or otherwise. So a whole new generation of recycled prophets have come to our rescue with the theory that we won't be here anyway, but we will have a seven-year sojourn somewhere into outer space until everything settles down again. It's a good idea, but there's only one small problem. It's not in the Bible. Not only will you fail to find "two or three witnesses" to verify the theory, but the honest student will not even find *one* witness without the facilitation of a talented text juggler. We've already touched on this in Chapter 7, but we didn't cite the origins. It's a relatively new conjecture, not yet 200 years old.

This clever idea of a "secret" rapture came from a so-so speculation generated about the middle of the eighteenth century by one J.N. Darby from the United Kingdom.[15] The theory was aided and abetted much later

---

13.　For multiple references see Bob Larson, *Straight Answers on the New Age Movement* (Nashville: Thomas Nelson Word, Inc. 1989), 218-219; Dave Hunt, *Peace, Prosperity and the Coming Holocaust,* (Eugene, OR: Harvest House Publishers, 1983), 65, 70, 72, 74; Constance Crumby, *Hidden Dangers of the Rainbow* (Los Angeles: Vital Issues Press, 1983).

14.　Lk. 16:8b KJV.

15.　James McKeever, *The Rapture Book* (Medford, OR: Omega Publications, 1987), 148. See also Marvin Byers, *The Final Victory: The Year 2000* (Shippensburg, PA: Destiny Image, 1994), Part II "When Does the Rapture Occur?" 55-123.

in life by the dispensationalist adventures of Dr. C.I. Scofield, whom we also met in Chapter 7. The marriage of ideas was unfortunately a convenient one and spawned no small shortsightedness throughout a large segment of the Church that you would think should know their Bibles a bit better.

As with any error of judgment, someone is always apt to experience a bit of the pain in one way or another, and in this case, the Jew cops it again. If examined carefully, the hypothesis bares yet another angle of anti-Semitism, and it needlessly puts our New Testament in a bad light to our Jewish family who need all the light—and love—they should be getting from their Christian brethren at this point in time.

But that's not the only damaging fallout. The constant repetition of this less than ingenious theory has been drummed to the point where ordinary souls no longer bother to check their Bibles or even think. It has been repeated with such vigor and intensity over the last half of this century that multitudes have taken it for "gospel truth," and they would not have the slightest clue what to do if their theory—like the stock market—collapses. Eventually we'll have a few more positive insights in Chapter 10 of this book.

And there is one more victim of this improbable hypothesis. That's the Jew who has already *recognized* Yeshua as his Messiah, many of whom have expressed to me personally their dismay at this yet "one more" display of "biblical" anti-Semitism. If Messiah should make two pickups, as goes this most improbable postulation, would the believing Jew feel accepted enough to go in the first lot with the Gentiles, or might he be more comfortable to tough it out with his brethren for the second round?

But there is a bit better news about this whole debacle. Increasing numbers of respected Christian leaders and top biblical scholars have reassessed their previous position and turned a corner in this grossly misleading presentation of the last days, or else they never adhered to the flimsily fabricated theory in the first place.[16]

---

16. McKeever, *The Rapture Book*, 83, 149-151.

Where Is the Body?

But lest we stray too far afield from our primary purpose to pursue a *Body*, we dare give no further attention to numerous other non-biblical assumptions that have served as a foundation for the flawed "double return" theory. But suffice it to say that the Gentile Church—or a large segment of it—had better do a bit more homework in the Scriptures, or alternately encounter the uncomfortable consequences of too little and too late.

Whether it be mathematical statistics, laws of physics or Bible verses, honest scholars don't juggle the data the way they like it. They take it as it comes. Consequently, the signals we desire to convey in this discourse are not spurious, but they are the consistent warp and woof in the tapestry of Scripture from Genesis to Revelation, reflecting God's unchanging plan for His relationship with mankind. We are told of one *family* growing together, of one *people of promise* yearning together, of one *Body*, or *bride*, watching for her Bridegroom, of *one covenant people* identified with her God, of *two sticks* now inseparably fused together, and yes, *two olive trees* grafted into one, waiting for their Lord to appear.

But wait! Those *two olive trees* have been ruthlessly chopped down, and we have been left with two dead bodies—or it would appear to be two—lying unburied in the filthy streets of iniquity. That is no place to leave them! Let us proceed to Chapter 10.

Chapter 10

Eschatology According to James

Now to resolve the alleged death of our two immortal *olive trees*, let's move into a bit improved domain of biblical accuracy. This happens to be the better, if not the more magnificent side of the saga. We have some very distinct escape scenarios that are from the Scripture and that contrast sharply with the flawed evacuation theory that rendered us something less than impressed in the preceding chapter. There are at least three clear models in the New Testament that demonstrate the Lord's shielding of His people during that last countdown of three and a half years, three and a half days, or three and a half whatever, during which time the formidable beast goes about to destroy our *two olive trees*. Incidentally, there is much speculation abounding on who this creature may turn out to be, so I would duly caution my readers that any theory older than a decade or so would be highly suspect and not worth wasting much time on. Nor will we further distract ourselves from the primary focus which we are herein pursuing. Rather, let us look to the Almighty for His covering.

When I board an aircraft, I become most disenchanted if not a little bored to go through all those safety announcements for the umpteenth time. On the other hand, as a believer of pursuing higher standards, God forbid that I convey to my fellow passengers an attitude of arrogance or slackness. And if my beloved wife is with me, she will also dutifully prod me to pay attention in exemplary fashion for the benefit of all the innocent spectators seated around us! Notwithstanding, I do know there are immense benefits behind all those safety announcements. So I have my own bottom line. As soon as I board the aircraft, I check under the seat to see if the life vest is really there after all. They don't even ask you to do that, and once I found that mine was missing! Then I check the safety card to make sure I know where the exits are. My duty to family, fellow passengers and even myself having been executed, I can sit back and relax! So at this point, may we now turn to the Grand Pilot for the location of His emergency exits—just in case!

I have located three such biblical exits so far. The first one is the protective sealing of God's servants on their foreheads. In Revelation 7, one angel who possesses "the seal of the living God"[1] calls across the cosmos to his other angel colleagues who have been assigned to execute judgment:

Do not harm the land or the sea or the trees until we put a seal on the foreheads of the servants of our God (Revelation 7:3).

And at this point, the 144,000 spiritual immunizations, as it were, were dutifully carried out. Moreover, we can see the encouraging results two chapters later in Revelation chapter 9 in that those sealed ones were covered with a very authoritative immunity against the demonic forces that were billowing out like smoke from the pit:

[The demons] *were told not to harm the grass of the earth or any plant or tree, but only those people who **did not have the seal** of God on their foreheads* (Revelation 9:4).

Now if anyone has any questions about the demonic rage that is slated to sweep the globe, I suggest you remove your rose-colored glasses to recognize from the media content of this age that the cover of the pit is already well ajar. We can anticipate that satanic-oriented affront from the local crime epidemics to international terrorism and unprecedented, so

---

1.   Rev. 7:2.

we call them, "natural" disasters will be an ever-increasing peril throughout an environmentally raped and morally corrupt planet.

So we highly recommend getting your "immunity seal" straight away. Possibly you need a booster immunization from last year—or was it longer? But they won't have them at the city hall, nor even at the church office. If you get down on your knees in the back closet, I'm sure you'll find an old one that grandmother may have dropped years ago. If not, just look up—better yet, reach up—and you'll be taken care of shortly. Your "immunity seal" will appear in the form of a relationship, not a system nor even a religion. My family all has them. They didn't hurt at all.

But wait a minute. I did mention that the angels had 144,000 applicants they dealt with, and that notorious number is a spiritual rugby ball—football, if you happen to be American—if I ever saw one. Now that number means everything to everyone. You might have even looked it up in the larger text to make sure you heard right. To some that's all the passes that will be available for the "big party," so if you're late too bad! I don't recommend being late, but not for that reason.

Others use it as their spiritual meat cleaver to chop apart Jew and Gentile in the Book of Revelation, but we already have enough Bible behind us to blow that one out to sea. But seriously, there are legitimate concerns for the proper interpretation of the numerically detailed and tribally catalogued list of the highly acclaimed 144,000. We should have a clear look at the text:

Then I heard the number of those who were sealed: 144,000 from all the tribes of Israel.

From the tribe of Judah 12,000 were sealed,
from the tribe of Reuben 12,000,
from the tribe of Gad 12,000,
from the tribe of Asher 12,000,
from the tribe of Naphtali 12,000,
from the tribe of Manasseh 12,000,
from the tribe of Simeon 12,000,
from the tribe of Levi 12,000,

from the tribe of Issachar 12,000,
from the tribe of Zebulun 12,000,
from the tribe of Joseph 12,000,
from the tribe of Benjamin 12,000 (Revelation 7:4-8).

Sure enough, there isn't a Gentile in the list. Not so fast! Are you sure? There are two monumental gems in the above text that we ought to be looking at.

First, if you recall the insights we gained back in Chapter 8 from our Jew and Gentile model of two sticks becoming forever one in the hand of the prophet Ezekiel, one stick was the stick of Judah and those tribes associated with him. That was a clear reference to that remnant of Jews we know today, many of whom have now been gathered back to Israel, their land of promise. And the other stick, the stick of Joseph and those tribes associated with him, was the alternate reference to the other ten tribes that have now been long since scattered to the winds—and that prophecy had never yet been fulfilled.

That is, it appeared not to have been fulfilled until we considered that "sister" prophecy from Zechariah that "...ten men from all languages and nations will take firm hold of one Jew by the hem of his robe and say, 'Let us go with you, because we have heard that God is with you.' "[2] It does not take an overly furrowed brow to reflect on how Yeshua has brought the Gentile believers into the Family of Abraham, Isaac, and Jacob, ten as it were from every nation, now regrouping into the vacancies of those ten tribes that disappeared. We note that the tribe of Joseph is prominently represented in the list above. And nine of the other lost tribes who were to have been reckoned with him are all listed as well. So where are they now? Where will they be come sealing time? It is beginning to come very clear. The list above looks like there are not a few of us Gentiles represented in the 144,000 after all!

But remember that we always like to have at least two witnesses before we buy anything from the Book. We must have a look at that mystifying 144,000 intrigue. Where does this number come from? A

---

2.   Zech. 8:23.

well-known observation is that the number 12 in the Scriptures quite consistently represents a governing authority or domain. We have, initially,
the 12 tribes of Israel. Ishmael, the controvertible heir of Abraham, also
had 12 rulers who were descended from him. We have the 12 disciples of
Yeshua, and the number had to be restored to 12 after Judas fell by the
wayside. And of course, these eventually came under the mantle of the
12 apostles. In the New Jerusalem we have the names of the 12 tribes of
Israel on the gates of the city, and the names of the 12 apostles on the 12
foundations of the city wall—24 in all.[3] One more model of Jew and Gentile interrelationship, if you please! This likewise relates to the 24 elders
who worshiped the Lord before the throne of the Lamb—logically 12
plus 12—another model of the Family as a unit.[4] So what does 144 represent? That gets pretty easy. It is the model of the redeemed Jew and
Gentile multiplied together. And 1,000? That is the Scriptural convention
for multitude. Thus 12 x 12 x 1000 is a precise figure of the entire
redeemed *Body*—the chosen of Israel multiplied by all the host of Gentile believers times multitude. And in this we have a mathematically
encoded representation of the exact theme of our book. So 144,000 is
God's shorthand for a head count. And ours? John gives it to us in the following verse:

> *After this I looked and there before me was a great multitude*
> *that **no one could count**, from every nation, tribe, people and*
> *language...* (Revelation 7:9).

My apologies forthwith for any or all cults, large or small, who
would limit the elect of the Kingdom to 144,000 souls. You may be asked
to move over!

And that was "Emergency Exit" number one.

A second covering scenario for the troubled times ahead is a prophetic allegory for a geographic isolation and thereby protective shield
over Israel. In Revelation chapter 12 we have pageant-like portrayal of

---

3.   Rev. 21:12-14.

4.   Rev 4:4; 5:8.

"...a woman clothed with the sun, with the moon under her feet and a crown of twelve stars on her head."[5]

In the allegory, she is pregnant and gives birth to a son. The devil who is characterized as an enormous red dragon attempts to destroy the child the moment he is born, but he is snatched up to heaven in the protective custody of the Most High. Careful study of the text leaves very little doubt but that the woman portrayed is Israel, and her son of course is our Lord Yeshua the Messiah.

The drama continues to unfold as the woman then flees "...into the desert to a place prepared for her by God, where she might be taken care of for 1,260 days"[6] The dragon then pursues her to destroy her, but she is "given the two wings of a great eagle"[7] where she is again carried to a place prepared in the desert for her protection. The devil again tries to sweep her away with a great flood, but a chasm opens in the earth to engorge the flood waters, and she remains high and dry. The dragon is thereby "enraged at the woman and goes off to make war against the rest of her offspring—those who obey God's commandments and hold to the testimony of Jesus."[8]

There are several details of this parable that must be carefully noted. First, the time frame for this drama is initially marked as 1,260 days, which of course translates to three and a half years, but it could also hold a dual representation of a much longer period. But the latter time frame of the vision is the literary expression "of times and a time and half a time," which is also figurative for three and a half years. We have already dealt with this. Time wise, these expressions may well refer to multiple incidents involving both the longer and shorter spans of measurement, since the Almighty's protective covering of His people has occurred more than once over the eons of history. So I refuse to get hung up on calculating dates and times. But the very significant essence of these "three

---

5. Rev. 12:1.

6. Rev. 12:6.

7. Rev. 12:14.

8. Rev. 12:17.

and a half" time frames is that the sheltering feature of Israel in Revelation 12 is running concurrently with the reign of terror of the beast in chapter 13, *as well as* the drama of his destruction of the *two olive trees*, which we left lying in the dirty street in the previous chapter!

The next point in the pageant to thoroughly grasp is when we're talking about His spreading His mantle over Israel, we're also talking about covering for those whom God has included to be a *part of Israel*. This of course is the very fiber of all we have been presenting thus far. If the Gentile Church inherits full rights in the promises, then the Gentile Church inherits full rights in the promises! The "divine insurance policy" covers us as well.

I would hardly suggest that our text is telling us that the physical land of Israel is the only place of security for *all* Abraham's family, but it is abundantly clear to me that in this allegory of "the woman clothed with the sun" the Gentile believer also holds a corresponding tenure, somewhere and in some way, under the shadow of the Almighty. Indeed, our text even indicates that the dragon was irate and "went off to make war against the rest of her offspring—those who obey God's commandments and hold to the testimony of Jesus."[9] Now that sounds like someone I know! But I am more than confident that as goes the attack of the dragon, so goes the sheltering umbrella of the living God.

To finalize this potent promise of protection, there is no better summary to both Jew and Gentile than one additional textual witness in the closing chapter of the Book of Daniel. The Ancient of Days pledges to His faithful servant Daniel:

> ...*When that time comes, your own people will be spared—all those whose names are found written in the Book* (Daniel 12:1 NJB)

This is now our second "Emergency Exit." The first was the seal of Almighty God upon the individual believer. And now Israel—and all

---

9.   Rev. 12:17.

who have been grafted into her—have a divinely assured hiding place to shield from the violence of the coming storm.

But before we head for "Emergency Exit" number three, we ought to first investigate a few basic facts about the long-predicted time of troubles that are soon to engulf the globe. Times are tough enough already, but unfortunately, from all appearances there is worse to come—much worse.

Yes, you know, I'm referring to the great tribulation. No, I'm *not* referring to *The* Great Tribulation! If you will carefully probe your Bible, the prophet Daniel spoke of "...a time of great distress such as has not happened from the beginning of nations...."[10] *Distress* is also translated as "trouble" or "anguish" in variant translations. Jesus was recorded twice, once by Matthew and once by Mark, as reiterating the identical dire predictions as Daniel.[11] The New Testament records His words in various translations *as great tribulation, great distress,* or *great suffering.* But, neither Yeshua nor the prophet ever expressed this time of unprecedented anguish with the definite article "the" to mark it as a specific event with definable time boundaries.[12]

But there have been certain less than helpful Bible scholars who have added an unfortunate "the" to mark this prophesied time of dire distress. Then out of sheer speculation, by putting their own thoughts into Daniel's head, they have deftly assigned a seven-year boundary to this time of unprecedented peril. The gloss has been swallowed so innocuously that in many Christian circles *"The Trib"* has become a household term—replete with implications that neither Yeshua nor Daniel ever proposed! And these implications have added to the blindness and impassivity of much of Gentile Christianity, leaving them with not a clue to what has already begun to formulate around us!

---

10. Dan. 12:1.

11. Mt. 24:21; Mk. 13:19.

12. In a quite different context from the discourses of Daniel and Jesus, the definite article "the" is used in connection with *tribulation* in Revelation 7:14 in most translations, but the past tense setting in Revelation does not readily lend itself to the assumption of a "time boundary" with use of the definite article.

Eschatology According to James

But now the third "Emergency Exit" exhibited for us by the King of the universe is absolutely the one that gets me the most excited—perhaps because it was a bit obscure for so long. I found it in the little Epistle of James no less!

Now the Book of James is hardly heralded for its eschatology, but right there it is in chapter 5:

*Elijah was a man just like us. He prayed earnestly that it would not rain, and it did not rain on the land for **three and a half years*** (James 5:17).

It seems like we ran into this enigmatic *three and a half years* somewhere before!

A few years ago when I was coursing through James, this well-worn eschatological time frame quite nudged my inner consciousness, and there were some priceless insights coming up. As we continue to reiterate, it makes little difference if these are real years, symbolic years, or years with ten percent discount. The significance is that it clicks into the exact same time code as that of the terrifying tenure of the beast, which also happens to run parallel to the promised time span of isolation and divine protection over God's covenant family—original or adopted. And how could we forget our *two olive trees* which are to unceremoniously lie dead in the street during that cryptic *three and a half* measurement? In this case it is *days* rather than *years*, but what is the primary message?

To adequately grasp this, one ought to be thoroughly familiar with the account of prophet Elijah's confrontation with Israel's King Ahab which begins in First Kings 16:29 and continues on through chapter 19, and I leave it with the reader for highly recommended background reading before going on.

King Ahab was a rather despicable number, and is recorded to have done more evil in God's eyes than any of the kings before him. In fact he holds the dubious honor of being one of only four kings of Israel that most rabbis concur were so corrupt and idolatrous they will never have the displeasure of bumping into them in Heaven. And if you have already read the suggested text, you may well decide that he may have even headed up that list of four. Ahab's big downfall was that he deserted the God of his fathers to marry the wicked Jezebel, a blood-letting, carnal, materialistic idolatress from pagan Sidon. To this day, she has remained a dyed-in-the-wool symbol of an idolatrous world system that has its own agenda and has no use whatsoever for any kind of an interfering God who may pose a challenge to the worship of either dollars or devils. So King Ahab married this cyanide capsule, and in no time at all, he became better at dabbling with the demons than she was. So the Lord called Elijah off the bench and sends him into the ball game:

Now Elijah the Tishbite...said to Ahab, "As the Lord, the God of Israel, lives, whom I serve, there will be neither dew nor rain in the next few years except at my word" (1 Kings 17:1).

Well that little message didn't bring the apostate Ahab all that much joy, but faithful Elijah maintained his *three-and-a-half-year* prayer contract with his God, all the while the evil king was trying to do him in. The good news is that for the three and a half years that Elijah was on the run, God looked after him very meticulously, beginning first in the utterly desolate Judean desert alongside the crystal brook of Kerith:

The ravens brought him bread and meat in the morning and bread and meat in the evening, and he drank from the brook (1 Kings 17:6).

But because of the prolonged drought, the stream eventually dried up and—would you believe it—the Lord then sent him off to Sidon, Jezebel's former launching pad! This had to have been due to more than a sense of humor. The Almighty exhibits not a little amount of braggadocio at times. And there in a suburb of Sidon, He led Elijah to a widow, *a non-Jew*, from the very tribe of this Jezebel who hated the prophet with a passion. And this sweet little old lady looked after Elijah and graciously fed him until many moons later Elijah again commanded the rains to fall and the crisis passed.

Eschatology According to James

Now this saga, this demonstration, of the God of Abraham's provision for the not-by-accident *three-and-a-half-year* interlude is colossal. This is both a *bona fide* precedent that also doubles as another allegory. In that entire *three and a half years* Elijah remained undetected. Old King Ahab never laid a finger on him!

But there's much more detail to the parable. As Moses represented the power of the Word of God, Elijah represented the miraculous authority of the Spirit of God. Both met with Yeshua on the mount of transfiguration.[13] Miracle-working Elijah has a wide acceptance of also being symbolic of the Holy Spirit age, the era in which the Gentile Church now breathes—or ought to be breathing. And should it still be necessary to yet underline that truth, James reminds us that Elijah was a man just like us![14]

Moreover, all but one of the humanistic "kings" of the earth today (Japan) who currently form the framework of the G-7, the conglomerate of seven world governments who juggle and dominate the world's economies, have been spawned from soil that once sent the message of Jesus Christ to the ends of the earth. I have no personal judgment for any of the prime ministers or presidents who rise or fall from within these governments, but one thing is indelibly clear. These nations themselves no longer swear allegiance to the God of Elijah. They bow instead to the materialistic god of Jezebel, and development of the global economy has become the "all in all." The rich are getting richer, and the Third World is becoming more devastatingly bankrupt. The same God has been discounted. The same Jezebel has been wed. How interesting! Might this have any relationship—even in part—with the description in Revelation of the beast most terrible, the beast that "just happens" to have seven heads?

But if you're a spiritual Elijah, wherever your God takes you—in a remote wilderness, under their noses in a Gentile city, or a God-fearing settler in Judea or Samaria—old Ahab can't touch you. This third "Emergency Exit" is quite like the other two, perhaps even a summary. Moreover, it is the clearest, most realistic illustration yet of the shielding the

---

13. Mt. 17:2-3.

14. Jas. 5:17.

Almighty has provided for all His family and how. Thus, we have not one, but three repetitions of how our Father plans to look after us.

As a word of caution, I would not be so simplistically naïve as to imply that no one will ever get hurt—or even killed. You could get killed in your automobile tomorrow, and not in a nice, bloodless manner at that. But our message from the Most High is that He has a plan. And if you subscribe to His coverage, you'll not have to worry.

So now let's go way back to our previous text in Revelation 11 with our two witnesses, our *two olive trees*, mercilessly overpowered and killed. And their dead bodies lie in the street for three and a half days. From the insights on the three variations of God's promised divine covering that we considered above, is it feasible that the Gentile believers along with Israel—as a *Body* scattered worldwide remember—are not all as dead as the world powers might hope? Does our allegory suggest that quite like Elijah under cover, might our *two olive trees* be down but not out for that turbulent three and a half years—or might it even be three and a half days, or whatever pre-ordained time frame a merciful Almighty has a perfect right to select? This likelihood has definite plausibility with the abrupt and jarring resurrection of the pair right under the very noses of the masses who had hardly finished the pretentious celebration over their presumed defeat:

> *But after the three and a half days a breath of life from God entered them, and they stood on their feet, and terror struck those who saw them. Then they heard a loud voice from heaven saying to them, "Come up here." And they went up to heaven in a cloud, while their enemies looked on* (Revelation 11:11-12).

Thus we automatically shift from the metaphorical to a long awaited prophetic reality as we will confirm in the texts that follow below. Sheer terror seizes the humanists of a new age that presumed that they had solved the problem of those "hardliners" who refused to cede their principles for the pursuit of worldwide peace, prosperity, and permissiveness. It was to have been an era where all would have their rights, except of course, for those few problematic ones who still revered the Bible. Oh, ye god$, what has gone wrong!

Do you suppose that our *two olive trees* were not quite as dead as the world system had presumed? In the jamming of their message with mass propaganda, the corrupting of their systems with syncretism, the banning of their Bibles as racist materials, and the crushing of their operations with the "human rights" of those who hated them had they—like Elijah—only slipped underground, and were only presumed to be dead by those who had become over-dulled by their newly established domain of peace and freedom? I believe I must leave that decision with you.

The above scenario of heading for an awaited Messiah that appears in the clouds is hardly a one-off prophecy. It is the *seventh* and final Scriptural prediction of what the theologians have since coined as the "Rapture"—the catching up of His Body to be gathered to Himself. The very first reference in the *Tanakh* appears in the prophecy of Zechariah—complete with the precursor events in Israel in the end of days:

Then the Lord my God will come, and all the holy ones with Him (Zechariah 14:5).

Take careful note that the venue of arrival is very specifically stated to be the Mount of Olives.[15] Yeshua is next to describe the long anticipated event. His prophecy is recorded three times, once by Matthew, once by Mark and again by Luke:

At that time the sign of the Son of Man will appear in the sky, and all the nations of the earth will mourn. They will see the Son of Man coming on the clouds of the sky, with power and great glory. And He will send His angels with a loud trumpet call, and they will gather His elect from the four winds, from one end of the heavens to the other (Matthew 24:30-31).[16]

---

15. Zech. 14:3-4.

16. See also Mk. 13:26-27; Lk. 21:27-28.

Where Is the Body?

If Jesus presumed to change the point of arrival from the Mount of Olives to New York or Geneva, He forgot to mention it!

Then Paul the apostle in his letters to the churches in Thessalonica and Corinth further details this identical but unique phenomenon, and thereby adds two more textual verifications—the fifth mention and the sixth mention—to the previous prophecies of Zechariah and Yeshua:

> *For the Lord Himself will come down from heaven, with a loud command, with the voice of the archangel and with the trumpet call of God, and the dead in Christ will rise first. After that, we who are still alive and are left will be caught up together with them in the clouds to meet the Lord in the air. And so we will be with the Lord forever* (1 Thessalonians 4:16-17).

And, last of all, is the above-cited scenario involving our *two olive trees*. Anyone who would dare to suggest that these seven consecutive descriptions of an identical event are not all pointing to one and the same arrival deludes himself with sheer fantasy. Nor could anyone but a pagan Roman Emperor—or possibly the likes of Chairman Arafat—ever seriously postulate that the point of arrival will be anywhere but Jerusalem.

And with that understanding firmly established, it becomes abundantly clear from the immediate context of Zechariah's prophecy, quoted above, that this rapturous happening has forever been planned to coincide with the Messiah's deliverance of Jerusalem from the long prophesied armies of *all the nations* who will endeavor to attack and devour Jerusalem at the end of days. Have you been following the world news lately? This very contemporary scenario has also been most graphically pictured by Zechariah:

> *I am going to make Jerusalem a cup that sends all the surrounding peoples reeling, Judah will be besieged as well as Jerusalem. On that day, when **all the nations** of the earth are gathered against her, I will make Jerusalem an immovable rock for all the nations. All who try to move it will injure themselves* (Zechariah 12:2-3).

112

Eschatology According to James

May we be reminded that Jerusalem not *only* happens to be the declared eternal capital of Israel, but as you may recall, it has been designated over 20 times in the Book of Deuteronomy as "...the place the Lord your God will choose as a dwelling for His Name."[17] Even if there are those who disparage the 3,000-year-old claim of the Jews, it is clear that there is a Title Claimant of even longer tenure than the Israelis who has vested interests in this particular real estate!

And then there is one more reinforcing parallel passage in the prophet Joel which on research will be found to be describing the identical event:

> *I will gather **all nations** and bring them down to the Valley of Jehoshaphat. There I will enter into judgment against them concerning My inheritance, My people Israel, for they scattered My people among the nations and divided up My land* (Joel 3:2).

The Valley of Jehoshaphat is one and the same as the Kidron Valley, just a few minutes outside of the Old City of Jerusalem, and which Yeshua routinely crossed to go to the Mount of Olives to pray. These days, however, it functions as a hotbed of hatred against the Jewish presence in and ownership of Jerusalem. The words of the prophets are now becoming very, very relevant!

And finally there is a third supporting text for the last battle for the city of the Great King. Zechariah again tells us what we can expect:

> *I will gather all the nations to Jerusalem to fight against it; the city will be captured...half the city will go into exile, but the rest of the people will not be taken from the city. Then the Lord will go out and fight against those nations, as He fights in the day of battle. On that day His feet will stand on the Mount of Olives, east of Jerusalem, and the Mount of Olives will be split in two...* (Zechariah 14:2-4).

---

17.   Deut. 12:11a.

And the finale of it all, the long-yearned-for advent of Messiah, is where we began above:

...then the Lord my God will come, and all the holy ones with Him (Zechariah 14:5).

In conclusion, Almighty God never violates His principle of requiring at least two or three witnesses for alerting us to anything of major importance, in some cases repeating His message up to ten times. And He has now demonstrated to us the three-stage parallel of his *two olive trees* all the way through the Scriptures to the bittersweet end. Mostly sweet, I should say, since we also have those three divinely ordained "Emergency Exits" to open up for us when the remainder of the planet goes mad.

And then one more reminder that our Father does not speak to us in one-off murmurs but in multiple messages. We have presented above a chain of seven distinct repetitions of our Messiah's magnificent return to His rightful reign in Jerusalem, drawing His redeemed to Him en route.

And in the final allegory of the *two olive trees*, we also see one additional illustration of the inseparable linkage of Israel and the rest of the *Body*, those Gentiles adopted into the family of Abraham through the mercy of Yeshua. At the time of my writing, tensions, suspicions and misgivings between the two groups appear insurmountable, but there are cracks beginning to appear in—if I dare conjure up one more word picture—"the Berlin wall of sanctified anti-Semitism." Who knows how fast the Most High might move in these days? The wise on either side must note just how much we need each other—God-fearing Jews and believing Gentiles—until our Messiah actually does appear.

Then, last of all, going all the way back to the impossible mountain that overwhelmed Zerubbabel, we have a clear-cut message that neither Jew nor Gentile has exhibited all that much unadulterated perfection when operating under his own self-styled sanctity. There is one and one only Judge. Neither can dare scorn, condemn, denigrate, or humiliate the other. As 12 elders from Judah along with 12 elders of the Adopted Ones

114

for a total of 24 elders, fall on their faces before the Lamb,[18] the message remains the same:

> ... *"Not by might nor by power, but by My Spirit," says the Lord Almighty* (Zechariah 4:6).

---

18. Rev. 4:4,10; 5:8.

Chapter 11

How "Saved" Is the Jew?

Are the Jews saved? How can an "unsaved" Jew be part of the *Body?*

That's a good question. We'll try to answer it. But first I've got a better one:

Is a Christian saved? We have baptized Christians, confirmed Christians, committed Christians, nominal Christians, born-again Christians, backslidden Christians, Lebanese Christians (as opposed to Lebanese Muslims), Christian Democrats in the parliaments of Europe, and Christian Scientists—as opposed to Christian scientists. Obviously parameters are in order, but once sufficient guidelines are in place, who makes the final evaluation? The whole situation reminds me of a rather prominent Rabbi we all know who said:

Do not judge, or you too will be judged (Matthew 7:1).

One of His foremost disciples reinforced that monumental instruction with:

Who are you to judge someone else's servant? (Romans 14:4a)

117

Where Is the Body?

My heavenly Father has taught me several basic principles over a goodly life span of ministry to His multifaceted family, and one of them is: The stronger my mental fixation on my friend as one "unsaved," the less efficiently will I ever be able to help him wrest free from his chains to prepare himself for the Kingdom of God.

And a second is not unlike the first: The more I behave toward my fellowman as if he were quality Kingdom material, the better are his chances of being transformed to the spiritual level that his Creator has designed for him to be.

So how does this relate to my Jewish family? To make a sweep of the most naïve mentalities, how did Abraham happen to make it without a proper Christian baptism? Obviously we find him quite prominently in Heaven in Luke's record[1] and in a somewhat similar heavenly backdrop when Jesus declared that Abraham got excited to see His birth.[2] Of course, we know—to express it in popular terminology that is used by a goodly segment of the Church—that Abraham "got saved" by looking ahead to his promised redemption in the atonement. Of course, this has a measure of theological correctness. But on the other hand, let's face it. Abraham knew a lot more about just listening to the Almighty than he did about Western theological interpretation. Yet I reckon God will forgive Abraham if he doesn't have his doctrine all sorted out as systematically as we do! When we all "gather 'round" the Throne of God, do you suppose we ought to let good old Abraham stay for the communion service or not?

And then it could be a jolt to some that Jesus was not really a Christian. He was an observant, orthodox Jew filled to an immortal capacity with the Spirit of His Father. He was "the Lamb of God who takes away the sin of the world."[3] The label Christian was hardly conjured up by our Lord, nor was it even in use in His day. It was coined long after His death

---

1.   Lk. 16:19-31.

2.   Jn. 8:56.

3.   Jn. 1:29.

118

and resurrection, and even then frequently used as a less than complimentary term to categorize Jewish Messianic believers in Yeshua.[4]

Now it follows that if Jesus was a Jew, His brothers and sisters were—and still are—Jews. He moreover obliquely reminded us in a well-known but frequently marginalized text in Matthew:

> *The King will reply, "I tell you the truth, whatever you did for one of the least of these brothers of Mine, you did for Me"* (Matthew 25:40).

His brothers were Jews, you know!

Without question, this also includes His adopted family from the Gentile world as we discussed in previous chapters. On one occasion Yeshua reinforced the concept of extending His immediate family when He made His actual blood family wait outside, while He continued to teach and heal others crowded within the house.[5] However, His pronouncement that those who obey His teaching have also become His family was hardly recorded to teach exclusion of blood kinship, but rather the equal inclusion of many others as family as well. But even at that, those outsiders-come-kinfolk at that particular gathering still happened to be all Jews at that point in time.

One more incident in context is exemplified by our Lord's dying prayer for the jealous, hate-blinded hierarchy from *some* of His own people who had pressured Pilate for His execution. It has been classic since Constantine to condemn all Jews over the centuries for the reckless curse an agitated, angry mob cried out on the day of His crucifixion, "Let His blood be on us and on our children!"[6]

Any sane, thinking person should know that this was hardly the cry of *all* Jews at the time, and certainly not those of the entire Diaspora in long ages to come. But even for this rebellious regime, Jesus' parting plea

---

4.   Acts 11:26.

5.   Mt. 12:46-50; Mk. 3:31-35; Lk. 8:19-21.

6.   Mt. 27:25b.

of compassion on their behalf was, "Father, forgive them for they do not know what they are doing,"[7] an ensuing blanket embrace of even those of His own flesh and blood who had betrayed Him. No sooner had it been uttered, than this mindless curse was canceled by the One who had all power in Heaven and earth to do so.

Jesus has never written off His Jewish family. Have you?

A very poignant encounter took place years ago in Wichita, Kansas, with newspaper reporters who were interviewing a former prominent Christian missionary to Israel. He had been asked by the Israeli government to serve as a spiritual counselor for Adolf Eichmann during his Nazi crimes trial in Jerusalem. Next to Adolf Hitler, Eichmann was regarded to be the most responsible Nazi criminal for the mass murders of six million Jews throughout Europe.

The reporters asked the missionary two questions:

"Do you believe the six million Jews, cruelly slaughtered by the Nazis went to hell because they could not accept Christ?" The missionary answered, "Yes."

The second question:

"Do you believe that if Adolf Eichmann had accepted Christ at the last moment, he would have gone to Heaven?" Again, the missionary replied, "Yes."[8]

It is not the Bible that does these things to our brains, but teachings, traditions, and theologians fueled with anti-Semitic interpretations. And if there is anything that I pray you get out of this book, it is to get out of your bias and into the Bible. It is actually a Jewish book, you know!

Most of us have no comprehension whatsoever of the hellish dimensions of Hitler's holocaust. Even having read the books or having wept

---

7.   Lk. 23:34.

8.   Elmer A. Josephson, *Israel, Key to God's Redemption* (Hillsboro, KS: Bible Light Publications, 1974), 79-80.

through the halls of the museums of remembrance, no one who was not there can ever sense the mindless insanity—nor can anyone who was ever forget! How could any Gentile deem himself qualified to pronounce a second infernal judgment on those who marched into the gas chambers singing *Anachnu Maamenim*, "We believe in our hearts...with perfect trust...in the coming of our Messiah"?[9] Never! Thank God, these are not the judges!

With an absolute certainty, the New Testament teaches consistently that our Lord Yeshua is the Father's sole provision for redemption of all humanity; there is no other access. His teaching is legendary:

> *...I am the way and the truth and the life. No one comes to the Father except through Me* (John 14:6).

Of that there is no question. Paul in his letters to the churches also repeatedly underlines the universality of the atonement:

> *For since death came through a man, the resurrection of the dead comes also through a man. For as in Adam all die, so in Christ all will be made alive* (1 Corinthians 15:21-22).[10]

But there are also those unmistakable pronouncements that the domain to judge another man's servant has never been left in my hands. In fact, I've been told quite clearly to keep my hands off! Moreover, self-centered arrogance may well dull our senses to the fact that the Architect of the Universe has reserved for Himself a few dimensions to the when's and how's of redemption that our wee intellects have never fathomed. Need we be reminded that there are not a few references in Scripture contrasting the wisdom of the Most High with our minute mentality? One of the most applicable for the occasion is:

> *...With man this is impossible, but with God all things are possible* (Matthew 19:26).[11]

---

9.   Josephson, *Israel, Key to God's Redemption*.

10.   See also Rom. 3:21-26; 5:18-19.

11.   See also Mk. 10:27; Lk. 18:27.

Where Is the Body?

A most valuable encounter of my own occurred many years ago with another senior missionary friend in Papua New Guinea. As I was sharing with her some of my evolving insights into what God was beginning to again establish among His chosen people who had returned to Israel, she responded impassively, "Yes, just as long as they receive Christ *before* He returns…"

It had only been an impromptu and informal exchange, and it was hardly in a setting conducive to a high-level theological interaction. I promptly dropped the matter. It was obvious she wasn't much into the trivialities of Jewish redemption!

Her indifference to the matter did a few flip-flops in my mind that day, then in the quiet of the evening the Lord quite unexpectedly nudged me in context, "What about My servant Paul?" Thus, driven to mentally scan the Word on the issue, the anti-Semitic shroud that tended to obscure bits of the truth for centuries began to unravel.

Saul-come-Paul was a violent hater of the early followers of Yeshua and was on a frenetic one-man campaign to lock them up or worse, when the hand of the Lord unceremoniously dislodged him from his horse on his way to Damascus to discharge some of these very deeds. He heard an ominous voice calling, "Saul, Saul, why do you persecute Me?" On inquiring of the identity of the unseen intruder, the heavenly stranger replied, "I am Jesus, whom you are persecuting."[12] At that point, Paul needed no further theological insights. He knew the Scriptures—the *Tanakh*—backwards and forwards. He was not only convinced of his error. He was already signed up!

Then the Holy Spirit began to run much more across my mental screen. After the crucifixion of Yeshua, *every one* of the big names in the New Testament needed a few visual aids to get their act back into focus. Look at brave and blustering Peter and all the rest of the now-faltering faithful, quivering behind bolted doors, fearing that they were the next in line for the chopping block! If these high-profile protégés of the Prince

---

12. Acts 9:1-19.

of Peace were supposed to be saved by faith, even the most die-hard would have to admit that they had precious little left. Precious little, that is, until Yeshua walks right through the wall and says, "*Shalom.*" Even then it took them a while to get restructured. And poor old Thomas who wasn't there for the first act, made the archives as the notorious doubter who needed a special replay of his own. The only difference between the faith of Thomas and all the rest was that he got caught by media watch![13]

Mary Magdalene sobbing in the garden was much the same,[14] as were the two other disciples who bumped into the risen Jesus on the Emmaus road.[15]

Suffice it to say that the elite of the New Testament all required a bit of visual boost to get them back on track, which a gracious Friend of Abraham seemed all too willing to supply. So with that divine precedent, what Gentile would have the audacity—not to mention the authority—to prohibit the Most High from again revealing Himself to His chosen remnant when His Messiah reappears to deliver them from the armies of the nations that are prophesied to surround Jerusalem in the presumably not too distant future?[16] But if this combination of Scriptural examples were not enough, we have one more very direct prophecy from prophet Zechariah, graphically portraying both the grace of Almighty God and the brokenhearted recognition by the remnant of Israel for their Messiah as He returns to Jerusalem:

> *And I will pour out on the house of David and the inhabitants of Jerusalem a spirit of grace and supplication. They will look on Me, the one they have pierced, and they will mourn for Him as one mourns for an only child, and grieve bitterly for Him as one grieves for a firstborn son* (Zechariah 12:10).

---

13.   Jn. 20:19-29.

14.   Jn. 20:10-18.

15.   Lk. 24:13-35.

16.   These and related prophecies for the battle for Jerusalem were detailed and footnoted in Chapter 10.

Nevertheless, the Christian Church since Constantine has held a heavy bias against any possible recognition of the Jew by his God if, at that particular point in time, he has no comprehension of or sensitivity to the sacrificial redemptive offering of the Lord Yeshua by His death. But is this truly biblical?

It is true that Paul had intense confrontations with many of his Jewish brethren both in Jerusalem and in the Diaspora as recorded in the Book of Acts. But did it include all the Jews? As we have already seen in Chapters 9, 10, and 11 of Paul's letter to the Romans, it most certainly did not.

In the beginning of Romans 10, he writes that his "...heart's desire and prayer to God for the Israelites is that they may be saved,"[17] which is a genuinely impassioned cry for the rebellious among his own people. By this was he saying that none of them at all were even looking in the right direction? Only those who have not finished reading the remainder of Paul's discourse on the subject might come up with that spurious conclusion. In fact, he completes his contention with a most unique declaration that "...all Israel will be saved":

> *And so **all Israel will be saved**, as it is written: "The deliverer will come from Zion; He will turn godlessness away from Jacob. And this is My covenant with them **when I take away their sins**" (Romans 11:26-27).*

In no way could this or any other text be used to justify any ignorant suggestion that ethnic heritage might constitute a license for iniquity. This is quite in league with the hypocritical claim that one's professed credo gives privilege to justify his ends with whatever means might suit his fancy—whether he be Jew, Christian, or otherwise. This naïveté ought hardly merit a mention, but unfortunately there are those among us who either reason along these channels or assume that others do.

To summarize the point, one would do well to recheck the Book he says that he believes in. One needs to make doubly sure his opinions are

---

17.   Rom. 10:1.

the same as those held by the Father of Abraham and not merely of the sincere but single-minded (read: one-eyed) traditions of the ancestors.

Once more we must reflect on Yeshua's parting assignment to His disciples. Going into *all the world* with the message of the Almighty's olive branch held out to the sinful pagan was directed initially to those who had no concept—much less a relationship—with the one and only Lord God of Abraham, Isaac, and Jacob. It is true that in Luke's Gospel narrative, as well as Luke's opening in the Book of Acts, He notes that the starting point is to be Jerusalem.

On one hand it would be utterly absurd to exclude our Jewish brethren from communicating good news of the atoning preeminence of their brother Yeshua. But on the other hand the Church—those who through the Messiah have been awakened, redeemed, and adopted into the family of Abraham—need to at long last wake up to the fact that the blessing that we ought to be sharing with our Jewish half of the family is radically different than the approach we should use toward an utter pagan. It is long past time that all pre-programmed mouthpieces of the Most High realize that a little homework is always in order and a tad of wisdom is never out of place!

Some of the seeds of this very insight evolved from the Catholic church as early as 1965 when sincere soul searching in Vatican II recognized that the Jew, after all, has a significantly deeper relationship to the Church than the adherents of such non-Christian religions as the Muslim, the Hindu, or the Buddhist. Pope John Paul II, himself, later expressed his own conclusion:

"Other nations have also suffered terribly, but the case of the Jews is special; they are the chosen people, they remain the chosen people."[18]

---

18. In a personal interview with linguist, Fr. Jochanan Elihai, as quoted in *Jews and Christians from Past to Future* (Cerf, 1990) in French; also the same title in English by Fr. *Elihai* (Jerusalem, 1997) unpublished.

Where Is the Body?

But the time span of Messiah's redemption is also of primary significance. This sacrificial blood offering reaches back as far as Adam. Looking forward, His grace spans eternity. Father Abraham, the Patriarchs, and their offspring were redeemed by looking forward to the promise—the Lamb of God that takes away the sin of the world. I am captivated by my redemption with each breath I breathe. It would be a stunning revelation to many otherwise learned Christians just how deeply many Jews—not unlike their ancestors—prayerfully yearn for their Messiah. Even more of a shock to the good old sectarian system is the genuineness of repentance before the eyes of their God, which they yearly pursue on *Yom Kippur*, the Day of Atonement. Yeshua, you should remember, is no stranger to the synagogue. They even used to call on Him regularly to teach there. They kept His Word in there—and they still do. Is it a wild-eyed assumption that He might still be there on *Yom Kippur* silently, obscurely taking note of a few of those more passionate prayers of repentance?

Do you remember the crippled man that Jesus healed at the pool of Bethesda? He had no idea who had touched him so incredibly until he ran into Jesus later at the temple.[19] Would it take that much backpedaling from prejudice to realize that the Jew who approaches his Father for forgiveness today might quite likely find out who atoned for it when he runs into Yeshua "tomorrow" in a temple that is yet to come? It boggles the mind how the Gentile sons of the Most High wormed their way into such an authoritative seat of judgment over some of their still struggling brethren.

We have already used the text earlier in the chapter, but the current context again bears repetition:

> *And I will pour out on the house of David and the inhabitants of Jerusalem a spirit of grace and supplication. They will look on Me, the one they have pierced, and they will mourn for Him as one mourns for an only child, and grieve bitterly for Him as one grieves for a firstborn son* (Zechariah 12:10).

---

19.   Jn. 5:1-15.

How "Saved" Is the Jew?

The Scriptures do seem to indicate that the God-fearing Jew who yearns for his redemption will not be disappointed at the advent of his Messiah, even though at the moment he may be entirely oblivious of what Yeshua has already provided.

But there's a lot more Bible to overrule some of the oversimplified anti-Semitic assumptions that many of us have grown up on. Another "witness" is the graphic cleansing of the high priest, Joshua, one more poignant allegory of Israel in Zechariah Chapter 3:

Now Joshua was dressed in filthy clothes as he stood before the angel. And the angel said to those who were standing before him, "Take off his filthy clothes." Then he said to Joshua, "See I have taken away your sin, and I will put rich garments on you" (Zechariah 3:3-4).

The rest of the metaphor continues with an exacting description of Israel at the end of days, and the Lord Almighty finalizes it with His inalterable promise:

...and I will remove the sin of this land in a single day (Zechariah 3:9).

And one more textual "witness" to the still to be finalized promise of redemption to *all* Israel presented by both Jeremiah and Ezekiel:

For I will take you out of the nations; I will gather you from all the countries and bring you back into your own land. I will sprinkle clean water on you, and you will be clean; I will cleanse you from all your impurities and from all your idols, I will give you a new heart and put a new spirit in you; I will remove from you your heart of stone and give you a heart of flesh, and I will put My spirit in you and move you to follow My decrees and be careful to keep My laws. You will live in the land I gave your forefathers; you will be My people, and I will be your God (Ezekiel 36:24-28).[20]

---

20. See also Jer. 31:33-34.

Where Is the Body?

There are not a few among us who could readily cite with precision accuracy the day, hour, and minute that they were saved. Moreover, many would also relate with vivid memory details of that very special encounter with their Lord. I will favorably appreciate knowing your testimony of the encounter, but I may have a small problem accepting your perception of the actual timing.

Perhaps we might consult Scripture to improve your accuracy of understanding when it truly did occur. That unforgettable day, hour, and moment that may be so outstanding was not really when the most indelible part took place after all. That just happens to be the time when *you* comprehended it!

For He chose us in Him before the creation of the world to be holy and blameless in His sight. In love He predestined us to be adopted as His sons through Jesus Christ, in accordance with His pleasure and will (Ephesians 1:4-5).

The final composition of the *Body* that has long been a monumental mystery to much of mankind, was no mystery to our Maker from the dawn of time. He alone knows whose free will choices will fall into place. We do not. Nor do we know when. The One who created the world's universal timepieces—the sun, the moon, and the stars on the fourth day of creation—seems to hold a different stopwatch from you and me. After all—if you are aware of the Genesis account—He had *light* on the matter already on that first day!

I had one of the most unforgettable encounters in my entire life when I went to share with the churches in Tahiti in French Polynesia a few years ago.

Several reporters showed up for a press interview scheduled with me on my arrival in Papeete, the capital. I suppose the significant pre-publicity of a representative from the International Christian Embassy in Jerusalem who was to speak on the relationship of Israel to the Church did attract some secular interest if not curiosity. A man appeared from one of Papeete's two main daily papers and a quite young, suave French lady from the other. A thirtyish blond lady represented Government Radio. She was the only one of the trio who managed any English.

The young French lady, through my host interpreter, questioned me first and began taking profuse notes. The man likewise took a few. She finally got around to asking why in the world would a Christian representative ever want to support the Jewish people? "We have the same God" was my summary reply. I did clarify what a true Christian sensitivity ought to be toward the horrific injustices that the Jews have suffered from the times of Pharaoh through Haman, the Romans, Hitler, and now the United Nations under the manipulation of pan-Arabic interests. I wound it up noting that the media also had little to display on its honesty ledger when it involves reporting on Israel, but suggested a hope that my three friends present might persist for a bit more integrity in their presentations!

The male reporter interrupted her briefly to further ask me a couple of short questions of his own and then promptly departed. The young French lady probed on, albeit her cynicism was obviously being tested to new elevations. With a few more queries she eventually wound it up. Catching the glance of the one remaining English speaking radio reporter, she rolled her eyes back in a this-guy-is-much-too-weird fashion and likewise took her leave. That left us alone with the blond lady from Government Radio. She had seemed relatively silent in the presence of the other two. In English, I began to add a bit more to the interview. Then for some unknown reason, I abruptly asked her, "Are you a Christian?" After a somewhat uncertain pause, she responded: "No...I'm Jewish!"

The ensuing three seconds of shock treatment simulated an eternity. She continued, referring to the two departed staffers, "You see how interested they are!" Her honest reflection of alienation effected an instantaneous identity in our spirits that words will never define. I added a few more details of my program, but really there was little more to say. I did add, "As a Christian, my message to you is to take your God seriously." My new friend replied, "I do."

She got up to go. In my abbreviated Hebrew I finalized, *"Baruch HaShem"*—Bless the Lord. She countered, *"L'Hitraot"*—See you again.

Where Is the Body?

In retrospect, reaching into the hearts of the Jewish people with God's eternal love in this their ultimate hour is slowly being rediscovered. This unique, if not powerful, encounter will far outweigh a thousand tracts on the Four Spiritual Laws.

In a wee epilogue, for the record, the male reporter actually gave me quite good coverage in the next day's paper. The alternate paper was conspicuously silent. I talked to my newfound colleague one last time on the telephone. She said she was going to air the details regarding my main seminar for the weekend. But that was purely academic. I have a hunch that if the Holy Spirit had any hand at all in setting this whole thing up— well, I hope to ultimately encounter that *L'Hitraot* in the Kingdom of God!

Western technical mentality more than manipulates even our ministry for God. The culture demands measurable results. It likes numbers and wants them now so the spiritual data base can be kept current along with everything else that sells big. It may come as a surprise to some that the Almighty doesn't reprogram all that readily—not even to the pet theories, programs, and assumptions of some of His sharpest kids!

How "saved" is the Jew? May we be assured that every Jew has a front row seat reserved for him in the coming Kingdom Praise Festival. Whether he ever shows up or not depends on his own priorities! In the meanwhile, as long as there's a question of whether he may or may not make it into the Kingdom, let's treat these V.I.P. brethren with the same respect their Father does!

Chapter 12

What Can I Say?

In 1995, Rabbi Eliezer Waldman, a highly esteemed, well-seasoned and awe-inspiring orthodox rabbi from Kiryat Arba shared in a seminar presented to hundreds of Gentile believers gathered from all over the world to attend the Christian celebration of the Feast of Tabernacles, the biblical *Sukkot*, which is sponsored annually by the International Christian Embassy Jerusalem.

His hometown in itself is an interesting place. Kiryat Arba is a biblical site and was the earlier name for Hebron, the locale of Abraham's first permanent roots in the land of promise. If the two settlements were not synonymous, they were probably located just across a sand dune from one another. The first mention of Kiryat Arba in the Bible was the recording of the death of Sarah, the wife of Abraham, in this very hallowed spot of Jewish history.[1]

Today, it is a restored Jewish community of no less renown. Adjacent to the largely Arab occupied city of Hebron, Rabbi Waldman's resurrected habitation is bitterly despised by its ethnic neighbors, and—along with many other Israeli towns throughout Judea and Samaria—incessantly barraged by world governments and media alike as "the greatest obstacle to peace."

---

1.   Gen. 23:1; see also Josh. 14:13-15.

Where Is the Body?

Not to worry. There are still a few Bible oriented Christians around who know Scripture well enough to appreciate who the original founder and title holder of Hebron was, and to whom the city still belongs today in spite of the foreign usurpers of the last century. Many of these faithful in their long hoped for pilgrimage to the Land of the Bible in no way want to miss a visit to Abraham's ancient Hebron and corresponding Kiryat Arba.

In this setting, a couple of Christian ladies occasionally involved in aiding such goodwill visits met and befriended one Gary Cooperberg, the Director of Public Relations of the orthodox *Yeshiva* (local Bible College) in Kiryat Arba. In the course of the friendship, they encouraged him to check out the work of the International Christian Embassy in Jerusalem. Now if one ponders the extremely unpleasant treatment the Jews have been dealt from Christians and Christian organizations over the last 2000 years, I would suppose this to be tantamount to suggesting that Daniel drop in to have a cup of tea with the lions when he had the time!

But Gary Cooperberg, being a godly man and of strong character, himself rose to the challenge and paid a visit. He came. He saw. He apprehended the opportunity. In due course of time Gary along with good Rabbi Waldman, his respected spiritual leader, was invited to speak at one of the Embassy seminars at the next Feast of Tabernacles. In their combined address, Gary opened with his initial impression of the unique gathering, "There is no questions in my mind but that the Presence of God is here." Further into his address, he reinforced this sensitivity in contrast to the utter spiritual barrenness of his own secular government, "When you go to the Knesset, something's missing; when you go to the Prime Minister's office, something's missing. I've sat in the halls of the Knesset and I've sat in the office of the International Christian Embassy, and I tell you, I feel the Presence of God more in the office of the Christian Embassy than in the entire hall of the Knesset."[2]

---

2. Rabbi Eliezer Waldman and Gary Cooperberg, from a lecture, *Issue of Hebron and Other Settlements*, given at the Christian Celebration of the Feast of Tabernacles, October 15, 1995, attended by the author. An audio tape of the seminar is available at the ICEJ office in Jerusalem.

What Can I Say?

Those who have preceived the power of Pentecost might well query, "How on earth can an orthodox Jew become privy to the Divine Presence?" Perhaps one might do well to adjust his vocabulary upward to say, "How in Heaven's Name can he know?" But already in the phrasing of our question do we have a built in answer!

What does the average Gentile believer know about the *Ruach Ha Kodesh*? Most Christians, including their leaders, know basically zero about an observant Jew's true spiritual life. Likewise, most Jews along with their rabbis, think in the same vacuum about a geniune Christian's real faith and convictions. Both sides are obviously more comfortable in stereotypes. The God of Abraham unquestionably has more far-reaching dimensions than mankind has a mind to measure. And His Holy Spirit, the *Ruach Ha Kodesh*, certainly has a far more significant web of connections than we have hitherto given Him credit. We all—Gentile believers and observant Jews alike—have much to learn from our common Father.

As we noted in Chapter 11, it is an exercise in extreme ignorance to categorize the God-fearing Jew within the pagan camp. Consequently, our relationship with our Jewish family ought to be, *and can be*, on a much different level of understanding than the ordinary godless unbeliever.

The first disciples were instructed to announce the good news to the pagan world, inviting them into the family of promise, and as the response would determine, to disciple them and to identify them with Yeshua through baptism. Those original disciples were Jewish, and there was never a question that they would not also introduce their own God-fearing brethren to their newfound Messiah as well. In fact, at the onset, due to hometown fever perhaps, *all* saw in their mandate a major focus on their own people. But their own people, though needing redemption as much as anyone else, were God-oriented and not pagan, and this would certainly present a difference in the approach. And unless God's promise to Abraham is to be buried in the sand, the ultimate end of the beacon was to flood the whole of the pagan world with light. This, of course, has since been taken as the long-standing commission of the Gentile believers.

Much water has gone down the Jordan river since those days, with the background panorama shifting significantly. The baton to reach the pagan with the message of God's love and redemption has largely passed from Jewish to Gentile hands. And in two millennia, the Gentile ought-to-be family has performed so despicably toward the Jewish people *and their God-given cultural heritage*, it is little wonder that the two groups have little left between them but an unbridgeable chasm of mistrust and the unassailable mountains of animosity. That's not exactly the way the Almighty had set it up!

These days there is again an increasing number of Jews emerging with a desire to share Yeshua among their own people. May the blessing of Almighty God be upon them! They have come to know their Messiah, and they have an inner ignition to share Him. It is realistic that they should have a bit more wisdom and integrity than their Gentile predecessors in embracing their own nation with the proper attitude, keener sensitivity, and a more meaningful approach. I hope they do.

But the Gentile Church by and large—and there certainly may be exceptions—finds their scenario shifted so drastically that we are driven back to the Scriptures to search for Plan B. No Jew wants a messiah who is unwittingly portrayed as one to uproot and destroy the rich Jewish cultural foundation that indeed stems from the very roots of the God of Creation. And no Jew is interested in a Jesus whose professed followers for centuries on end have re-pilloried them on a fictitious cross of hatred that was initially intended to save.[3]

Now, as the world is drifting steadily downhill toward an apocalyptic nightmare, we do find a few directives in the Word of God with regard to Jew and Gentile relationships that haven't been used all that much over the last 2,000 years. Having misunderstood, misapplied, and all too often, brutally misused the Great Commission with regard to the Jewish side of the family, it might just be the time to take inventory and start over. It is not that the Jew has not heard about Jesus, but unfortunately the scions of Constantine & Company seem to have presented the wrong one! With the few days (or is it hours?) that we have left, it's time that those of us Gentiles who know Him, desist with our preaching and begin to demonstrate what the real Yeshua is like!

---

3. For the shocking account of the violent crimes committed by the Church over the centuries in the name of God against the Jewish people, see Michael Brown, *Our Hands Are Stained With Blood* (Shippensburg: Destiny Image Publishers, 1992).

What Can I Say?

The Scriptures give the Gentile believers three specifics that we are instructed to express in our relationship toward our Jewish side of the family. First and foremost, we are to love them. Loving anyone from our enemies on up hardly needs any overt scriptural verification, but above and beyond that, there are numerous specific scriptural calls for Gentile believers to confirm their love with material assistance along with various other deeds of gratitude to their fellow Jews who were hurting from persecution at that particular time.[4] Loving kindness rarely goes unwarranted in the Kingdom!

An Israeli friend once confided to me that her Jewish people simply didn't know how to handle genuine love by an outsider. They have had to keep their balance for so many centuries in a sea of hatred and mistrust—and most of that by so-called Christians—that when someone drops in from another planet, as it were, to show them positive acceptance, they literally melt. Since that wee testimonial, I have seen this inescapable truth reflected over and over and over again in my not infrequent encounters.

Secondly, we are commanded to pray for our Jewish family. We are of course encouraged to pray for all men everywhere.[5] Praying, like loving, scarcely needs scriptural documentation. But again specific references to pray for the Jews collectively is the proclamation to pray for their ultimate redemption by employing the metaphor of Jerusalem. This is indeed a most relevant prayer burden for all who believe the Bible in these turbulent times. Jerusalem is the one and only city on the globe that is inseparably intertwined as a figure of the eternal Jewish destiny:

I have posted watchmen on your walls, O Jerusalem; they will never be silent day or night. You who call on the Lord, give yourselves no rest, and give Him no rest till He establishes Jerusalem and makes her the praise of the earth (Isaiah 62:6-7).[6]

---

4.   Acts 11:29-30; Rom. 11:18,20; 15:27; Gal. 2:10; and previously cited Mt. 25:40.

5.   See Eph. 6:18; 1 Tim. 2:1.

6.   See also Ps. 122:6.

Where Is the Body?

One need not overextend himself with an excessively furrowed brow to understand why there is such an international line of aggressively anti-Semitic suitors quarreling in the queue for Queen Jerusalem these days!

And finally, in his letter to the Romans, Paul the Apostle nudges the Gentile believers in Yeshua to instill a sense of a healthy, if not creative, envy among our Jewish brethren:

> *Again I ask: Did they stumble so as to fall beyond recovery? Not at all! Rather, because of their transgression, salvation has come to the Gentiles to make Israel **envious**...I make much of my ministry in the hope that I may somehow arouse my own people to **envy** and save some of them. For if their rejection is the reconciliation of the world, what will their acceptance be but life from the dead?* (Romans 11:11-15)

It is an absolute paradox! The Gentile Church has been given a most minimal assignment on what she ought to be doing toward her Jewish counterpart in the family of Abraham, yet her achievement rate has been something less than dismal. But even poorer results than that were accumulated in doing what she was never asked to do—to treat the Jew as if he were a godless pagan.

It would be well at this point to ponder the semantic difference and consequently the vast gulf between holiness and righteousness. Holiness is God's stamp of ownership on a person or a people—on a place or on a thing. Righteousness is God's standard. Holiness can be corrupted. A holy temple may be desecrated. A holy instrument may be defiled. A holy man or a holy people may become stained with sin. A once-holy object may become unusable. It may be discarded. Or it may be broken off and burned. Righteousness on the other hand is inalterable. It is God's unbending measuring stick. Righteousness is to become honed to the image of God. It is to become like God.

The Jews are God's holy people—along with those Gentiles grafted into their olive tree. The branches, the Scriptures tell us, may be broken off, God forbid, from either side of the tree. They are the chosen ones, stamped out, set aside for His purposes. Righteousness, however, is God's intention to transform His marked-out ones, first into His likeness, then into His presence. The more we understand God, the less likely we will be to try to play God.[7]

The specifically mentioned and most appropriate tool to relate to our Jewish family has ironically been the least used. Consequently, the Church in nearly 2,000 years has done dismally in making the Jews jealous in the positive dimension of the meaning. Those who regarded themselves as Christians have accused the Jews, cursed them, killed them, run them out of town, and have done an extraordinary job of driving them mad; but they have done precious little to make them jealous.[8] Humility toward the Jew as a chosen one of the Most High, an expressed appreciation for the Book He gave the world, a true brotherly love to ignite a spark for emulation has been virtually non-existent.

I was on my second trip to Israel, and the land at that time was still more of a nostalgic dream than it was the awesome replay of history that I sense it to be today. I found myself sitting next to a young Israeli university student as our bus ground up the western slopes of the Judean Hills into the city of Jerusalem. I heard her making a comment about her studies to a friend across the aisle which alerted me to the fact that her university major was identical to that of mine many years ago—the chemical sciences. And on that note, we began a conversation.

The opener soon shifted. She was an Israeli who lived about a half an hour out of Jerusalem, and being quite used to tourists, promptly sensed that I was a visitor all effervescent with the unique experience of Israel. The International Christian Embassy Jerusalem, which annually attracts some 5,000 visitors for the *Sukkot* holidays, was not all that well-known in those days, and I doubt what she knew of my specific purpose in being there. Regardless, she was automatically aware of the tourist-type ardor of my present setting.

She countered my fervency with, "You visitors get all excited about Israel, but you don't know what it's like to live here! They (the Palestinians)

---

7.   Ps. 50:21.

8.   Again, we would cite Michael Brown, *Our Hands Are Stained With Blood*, for a documented history of detailed crimes against the Jews by professing Christians.

would like to destroy us, and we young people would go somewhere else if we could, but there's nowhere for us to go."

At this, I promptly overflowed with quotations from the ancient prophets. I asked her if she knew the prophecy of the dry bones in Ezekiel chapter 37. After getting the prophet's name properly pinned down—the pronunciation of Ezekiel comes out starkly different in Hebrew—she most surely knew the much-renowned prophecy. I continued on with, "God has His umbrella over this place. Certainly there has been and will be trouble, but He has brought your people back to bless you, to keep you, and to cover you with His protection. This is your land forever!"

I get a mite spirited when I sense the prophetic fulfillment encompassing His land of promise, and this occasion was undoubtedly no exception. My enthusiasm must have bubbled over.

The young lady, looking at me with eyes expressing the yearning in her heart, responded, "I am *jealous* of your faith!"

She knew the vision in Ezekiel, but hardly knew Paul—and for sure not where he said:

*...I make much of my ministry, in the hope that I may somehow arouse my own people to **envy**...* (Romans 11:13-14).

A similar experience occurred a few years ago on a visit to Tahiti, the main island in French Polynesia in the South Pacific. My host had made an appointment for me to meet the president of the synagogue in the capital, Papeete. I wanted to let him know of our support and interest in his people, fill him in on my teaching program in behalf of Israel throughout the city's churches and to build friendship bridges in general. But as is almost cultural throughout the Pacific Islands, we unfortunately arrived a bit late.

The president also happened to be a very busy medical doctor in the Papeete hospital and on our arrival at the little coffee shop, my first question was to ask how much time he could spare. Glancing at his watch, he replied courteously, "Well, not really very much."

What Can I Say?

I knew that I therefore must be concise and quite collected. I gave him a brief overview of our purposes in visiting Tahiti, and as I frequently open with any new Jewish friends, I added an oblique apology to God's chosen people in general for the dismal record over the centuries of how miserably the Christian Church has misrepresented our Lord. "We're Christians, but with a significant difference from what you may have ever encountered before. We respect and support the Jewish people and have come to awaken the churches of Papeete to what a genuinely Christian attitude toward our fellow Jews ought to be like."

And then the Holy Spirit gave me an impromptu utterance that I have found to be an ultimate of accurate expression, "Whoever Jesus was, He brought me into your family!" It touched him. "What can I say?" was his deeply felt response.

From then on, the very busy young doctor didn't seem to be in all that much of a hurry. He stayed and stayed and stayed some more. There were a number of convenient openings in the conversation where he could have taken his leave. But he didn't. It seemed that we had many things to catch up on. Obviously, when you haven't had a good chat with your "brother" for a long, long time, no one really wants to dash off too quickly!

Without question, we should all prayerfully yearn for our Jewish family to be brought closer to their God and, through Yeshua, to experience the righteousness that has been reserved for them from the beginning of time. I ought to yearn for them to be filled with the Spirit of God as I have been filled and to sense a relationship with my Lord as I know Him. I would choose this not only for my Jewish friends, but for any and all!

But in this context, there is somewhat of a tinny if not hypocritical ring to the conventional mentality of "converting" the Jews. Is it an air of spiritual condescension that may be included? Is it the motive involved? Or is it sheer ignorance of what the Almighty already has given to His chosen people in contrast to what they do not yet perceive? If so-called "conversion" is only to get him to reject his Jewishness and shift his doctrines to ascribe to a Gentile Jesus that may be presented more as theory than reality, then one has indeed lost the plot.

Where Is the Body?

If one's assumed Gentile superiority bids him to enlighten his Jewish counterparts in doctrines of preferred "Christian teaching" over "outdated" *Torah*—he deludes himself. Most Christians have not the slightest inkling of the intimacy the practicing Jew has to the very same Scriptures of which Jesus declared that not even the tiniest particle would ever be deleted. He becomes a meat cutter hoping to advise the surgeon! For God so loved the world He offered our only hope on a Jewish foundation!

Or could it be the Christian's "saving faith" that is most likely to impress the Jew? In comparison with the faithful dedication of an obedient Jew to the God of his fathers, many a well-meaning Christian in this instance may appear as a raw recruit attempting to advise his commanding officer. All too often that which is naïvely postulated as "saving faith" is but another legalistic link to a body of doctrine—hardly a personal intimacy with the only One who can actually save.

But the demonstration of a pragmatic faith in the Most High, that fears not to confront the tidal waves of expediency is the kind of faith which the Jew waits to see—as does the whole world for that matter. A weeping humanity waits in desperation for a few more positive exhibitions from the multitudes who call themselves the Church, but demonstrate little genuine trust in anything they cannot touch or hold. Even less do they demonstrate a lifestyle that suggests any actual belief in the dire biblical warnings for the "end of days," which now appear to be upon us.

The faith that saves is the kind of trust that reflects an intimacy with our God. That would indeed propel our Jewish brethren to envy. But how can one reflect something he doesn't actually have?

And the greatest attraction of all is genuine love. Love is anything but a gushy, gooey, pandering, or paternalistic condescension. It is an unfeigned horizontal acceptance. What of the estranged and disillusioned child who has never known the real love of his mother—the resistant one who has never experienced the warmth from another? He cries for acceptance and not a lecture—a blessing and not a beating. What of the chosen of God who has endured condescension at best, and an Esau-like fist at worst, from those who should have been his brothers? The need for healing is quite the same.

What Can I Say?

The Papua New Guinean Christians who come up to Jerusalem for the annual Feast of Tabernacles are generally a brightly colored lot, not to mention their relaxed and radiant smiles that they tend to scatter around the city.

A few years ago, the delegation must have made a high-profile impression on one of the other guests in the dining room of the small hotel where we customarily stay. The middle-aged Jewish lady from America had apparently inquired from our hotel manager where all these sparkling Islanders had come from. He replied that they were Christians from Papua New Guinea who organize a group to come up to the Feast of Tabernacles every year to bless Israel. He further advised her that their leader was out in the lobby and that she might come out to speak with me, and so she did.

Our group was slated to depart within minutes, and I hardly had time to talk to her. But I gave her a fairly standard introduction to who we were and what we were about: "We're Christians for sure, but not quite the kind that you probably have heard about. We love the Jewish people and have come up to bless and support Israel. We believe that this is truly the Land that God has given you and we want to encourage you. Moreover, we want to thank you for your God and your Bible. We appreciate what all the Jews have given to us." It was, of necessity, quite an abbreviated fly past.

Then out came one of those impromptu gems of the Holy Spirit who induced me to say, "By the way, what's your name?" And her ready reply, "Ruth!"

My instantaneous response, "Indeed, and 'Your people will be my people and your God my God.' "[9]

She had on sunglasses, and I couldn't see her eyes, but her face revealed it all. Only the tears themselves were obscured by her shaded glasses.

That divine encounter in the hotel lobby brought Ruth closer to reality than 1,000 tracts in her mailbox. Moreover, I know that the Holy Spirit

---

9. Ruth 1:16b.

alone initiated that contact, nor will it be His last until that day when this daughter of Zion eventually meets her Messiah face to face.

A similar incident occurred on another occasion with yet another Papua New Guinea contingent that had come up to Jerusalem for the Feast of Tabernacles. We were again on the broad plaza below the Temple Mount where the faithful come to the Western Wall to pray. And because of the constant threat of terrorist activity by Israel's enemies, there are always a few soldiers around to keep an eye on the peace.

Now soldiers are supposed to be tough, and soldiers with guns would appear even more rugged yet. So there he was, a young, red-headed Israeli soldier sitting there with his rifle across his knees on guard duty not far from the *Kotel*—the awesome, last-remaining remnant of the second temple. This young man wasn't really the roughest looking soldier I had ever seen, but in his position of authority, he was formidable enough.

And here we came—bright colored and cheerful happy-to-be-in-Jerusalem Papua New Guineans. He couldn't help but notice us. After all, he was supposed to be keeping an eye on what was happening, and right then it was Papua New Guinea! I approached him with the usual, "We're Christians from the South Pacific. I don't know what you know about Christians, but we're not that kind. We're different; we love Israel, and we've come up to Jerusalem to bless you."

Then for some reason—I always recognize the Reason after the fact—I said to him, "You know that the prophet Zechariah said that in the last days ten from every nation will take hold of the coat of a Jew and say, *'Let us to go with you, because we have heard that God is with you.'*[10] Well, here we are!"

Rifle or no rifle, a big old tear started coursing down his cheek. Of course, he knew that Scripture! He'd likely heard it from the Rabbi or possibly learned it in school— or both. Anyway, there was no question that he knew it. But he'd never heard it from a *goy* before and certainly not from a Christian!

---

10. Zech. 8:23.

What Can I Say?

There is no question in my spirit that the Almighty will use this encounter and others of His design to shape that young soldier's destiny in days and years to come. If there truly is a Holy Spirit, and if He is as unique and mighty as we claim Him to be, He has hardly initiated these rare rendezvous only to create a good story. I am merely an agent to be available, a clay pipe to channel the Water of Life. He is the one who ultimately weaves the pattern together. Moreover, if we've tried by our own techniques to "witness" for 2,000 years with hammer and tongs, perhaps it's time we tried some jeweler's tools. In the meanwhile, a world—which includes our Jewish brethren—weeps silently for the revelation of an unfeigned intimacy with its God.

Chapter 13

Prophecies Near and...Far-Out

The most significant, far-reaching controversy of global implications in our day, and which at the very moment of this writing is surging toward a crescendo, is, "Who owns Jerusalem?" On December 4, 1996, the United Nations General Assembly voted by a majority of 148 to 1 that the "Israeli jurisdiction over Jerusalem is invalid and therefore illegal."[1] Need it be said that the lone dissenting vote was cast by Israel? And with a mention of Jerusalem some 800 times throughout Scripture, and 16 of the Old Testament prophets predicting God's restoration of Jerusalem to her former glory in the closing age of human history, need it be further mentioned that the Almighty doesn't quite see eye to eye with the United Nations? The Bible is unmistakably clear, making this political jockeying for sovereignty over Jerusalem in our time more than awesome. The explicit accuracy with which God's prophets spoke over 2,500 years ago is well beyond the statistical boundaries of happenstance.

But before we go to the whole of Jerusalem, let's have a brief look at the greatest focal point of contention in the whole of the city—the Temple Mount. There on the ruins of Solomon's glorious temple are

---

1. "UN Bashes Israel Over Jerusalem—Again," *Middle East Intelligence Digest*, Vol. 8, No. 1, Jan. 1997, 2.

positioned two Muslim mosques. Solomon's original temple was destroyed by Nebuchadnezzar on the ninth day of the Jewish calendar month of Av in 586 B.C. and was, some 70 years later, rebuilt by Zerubbabel, whom we met in Chapter 9.

Zerubbabel's spartan structure served its purpose until Herod the Great, in an effort to impress his Jewish subjects, remodeled it. This was the magnificent temple in existence during the time of Jesus that was, in turn, destroyed by Roman Emperor Titus in A.D. 70. Incredibly precise with respect to timing, this second catastrophe again occurred on the now most infamous date on the Jewish calendar—the ninth of Av![2]

Then came the mosques. Somewhere over the very site of God's Holy of Holies the eye-catching, glittering gold Dome of the Rock was erected between A.D. 692-697[3] and in the near proximity, the El-Aqsa Mosque was begun in A.D. 705.[4]

When the Old City fell back into Jewish hands in the miraculous Six-Day War of 1967, Israelis from rigid Orthodox to hosts of the most secular, from bearded rabbis to uniformed paratroopers, generals, diplomats, and government ministers converged upon the ruins of their sacred heritage at the base of the now Muslim occupied Temple Mount. Together they prayed, wept and rejoiced at the massive Western Wall foundation stones, the last observable vestige of the once glorious second temple.[5]

But Israel didn't touch the mosques. They relegated the upper Temple Mount to the authority of the Muslim Wakf. To this day no Jew nor Christian dare enter the sacred Temple Mount area to pray at the risk of a calamitous slur to Allah, which might easily result in riots of unmentionable

---

2. *Encyclopedia Judaica*, Vol. 3 (Jerusalem: Keter Publishing House, Ltd, 1971), 935.

3. Menashe Har-El, *This is Jerusalem* (Los Angeles: Ridgefield Publishing Co., 1981), 329-332.

4. Har-El, *This Is Jerusalem*, 53.

5. "Premier, Chief Rabbis pray at Western Wall," *Jerusalem Post*, Vol. 37, June 29, 1967. See also Collins and Lapierre, *O Jerusalem* (Hemel-Hempstead, U.K.: Simon and Schuster, 1972), 656.

proportions.[6] Obviously the deity of the Muslims is quite insulted by the God of Abraham, Isaac, and Jacob, so may we never be confused by the secular media or equally ignorant churchmen who unwittingly interchange the name of Allah with the God of the Bible. It would appear these two may not be the best of companions, nor will they ever be!

To the agony of the God-fearing Jews, the successive governments of Israel have been content to lapse into procrastination: *If it ain't broken, don't fix it!* Interfering with the mosques in any way shape or form would be tantamount to inciting *jihad* or Islamic Holy War and could theoretically ignite an uncontrollable militia of immense proportions, inciting volunteers from the coasts of Morocco and Mauritania in West Africa sprawling across to Indonesia at the edge of the Pacific rim. The giant Islamic serpent comprises something like 1.2 billion adherents to Allah worldwide and spans nearly half the globe. With this very real scenario, an impromptu army of 200 million as foretold in Revelation is well within comprehension.[7] But at this writing the mosques still stand for all to see and ponder.

Jesus in quoting the prophet Daniel, however, made a very intriguing comment:

> *So when you see standing in the holy place, "the abomination that causes desolation," spoken of through the prophet Daniel— let the reader understand—then let those who are in Judea flee to the mountains. Let no one on the roof of his house go down to take anything out of the house. Let no one in the field go back to get his cloak* (Matthew 24:15-18).[8]

Understand it if you can! Not a few have attempted the challenge, but I fear it may have been for the wrong reasons. The text sounds much more like an evacuation to be taken seriously rather than an ego trip for

---

6. "Get off the Temple Mount!" *Middle East Intelligence Digest*, Vol. 5, No. 9, September 1994, 4-5.

7. Rev. 9:16.

8. See also Mk. 13:14-16; Dan. 11:31; 12:11.

Bible cryptologists. Never mind reality. There have been a few proposed theories over the ages, including one currently popular postulation in some biblical circles, that those mosques *must* come down so that the Jews can build a *third temple*. Why? So that the "Antichrist" can thrust himself within the holy place in order to effect the above predicted abomination. That's all very good except for a few "Swiss cheese" observations. First of all, *antichrist* is mentioned nowhere in either the Book of Daniel or Revelation. Perhaps they mean the beast, but if they do they should say so.

The term *antichrist* is only used four times throughout the entirety of Scripture and that being in the Epistles of John, with the apostle's conclusion that *he* (the antichrist) is actually *they*, and that this multiplicity of spirits affronting the Messiah was already abundant in those days.[9] So to presume a singularly personified *Antichrist* in the end of days is most certainly treading on the thin edge of conjecture. This is hardly to suggest that the beast most terrible who—predicted both by Daniel and by John in the Book of Revelation—will ultimately confront the globe with humanistic tyranny, would ever fit into a robe (or is it robes?) of righteousness![10] But at least let's try to keep our terminology biblically correct.

So what of those mosques? Well, they've been around for quite a long while now, like between 1,290 to well over 1,300 years depending on when the construction was begun, when it was finished, or when they were dedicated to Allah or perhaps even on who happened to be marking the calendar? There was no question that in the days of the erection of those mosques the Jews were no more welcome than they are today. Little has changed in that respect. But the bottom line is that if there is anything that is an abomination to the Lord of Hosts, one can comprehend nothing more defiling, nothing more desecrating, than bowing in idolatrous reverence before His arch enemy of all time—and that on a location just above the Holy of Holies!

And should anyone wonder of the degree of desolation to the land of the Bible since the birth of Islam early in the seventh century after

---

9.   1 Jn. 2:18,22; 4:3; 2 Jn. 1:7.

10.   Dan. 7:7; Rev. 13.

Christ, one need only consult any pre-1948 reference text on the subject. We have already quoted Mark Twain in an earlier chapter, but archaeologists, clergymen, theologians, government statesmen, professionals of many backgrounds plus ordinary pilgrims have all given similar bleak accounts of a land once regarded holy.[11] That the land had changed its god was hardly without the dire consequences of desolation! An extremely informative, insightful, intensely researched and meticulously documented book on the effects of Islamic influence on what has been called Palestine for the last 1,300 years is *Philistine*, the text just cited by Ramon Bennett; it covers a wide range of the social, religious, and political fabric that has enshrouded the land for the 12 centuries preceding 1948.

Unfortunately, in the last several decades, there has been some mischievous tampering with previously recorded historical facts in encyclopedias, journals, high school and university reference texts used throughout the western world.[12] Since the rebirth of Israel in 1948, those who have loathed her existence have infiltrated news rooms, editorial offices of academic texts and periodicals, and consequently the classrooms. Those who are not familiar with the Bible would never know that there ever was a 4,000-year-old nation called Israel, and you can be sure that this Holy Book is now quite high on their hit list.

So let's pick up again on those two mosques and their consequences. The physical landscape of pre-1900 "Palestine" certainly had won no prizes as we have seen. What about the spiritual blessings of Islam? We won't waste too much time on that one from its impact on the Jew to the Christian to the World Trade Center! Could it be that the "abomination that causes desolation," given a bit of high profile by both Daniel and Yeshua, could have anything to do with the mosques? The closer we get to the final action, the clearer the total picture will become.

---

11.   Ramon Bennett, *Philistine* (Jerusalem: Arm of Salvation, 1995), 147-150.

12.   Ruth Willers, "The Palestinian Agenda in the New 'Britannica'," *Jerusalem Post*, March 26, 1993; See also "Britannica Redefines History," *Eye on the Media*, *Jerusalem Post International Edition*, April 1993.

Interestingly enough, Daniel spoke of the duration of the phenomenon of desolation as 1,290 days,[13] which is not unconventional in biblical scholarship to be understood as years. In fact it is very conventional. Moreover, we previously ran into 1260 days in chapter 11 of Revelation, which are not exactly the same, but are intriguingly similar. Nevertheless, the construction dates involving the two mosques—both of which are different—plus the other unknowns noted above, make the whole beginning picture fuzzy enough that one should not be overly tempted to get his calculator out. But to those who will do so regardless, please be advised that the Almighty has a tendency to be intentionally cryptic for amateur date setters. We may note again that those who give a higher priority to calculations than to intimacy with the Most High may well do themselves and others more harm than good.

Moreover, the primary purposes of our discourse are to expose phony theories that are something less than biblical and to get the more serious believers headed into the direction of the things that are. We must clearly recognize the presently emerging scenario, which had been long foretold by the ancients for our day. And, above all, we want to get on with our scriptural search on *Body* building! Thus, I am quite content at this point to leave the oft-elusive numbers game to others.

Nevertheless, it does appear that Daniel's numbers are well within the ballpark, to help identify the "abomination that causes desolation" for our current insights. First and foremost, with a "temple desecration" already in operation for well over 1,260 years, it relieves us of all that hard work of having to build a third temple just so some Mr. Nasty can go in and mess it up!

Secondly, with no third temple construction to hold Him up, Messiah could just get back here before you know it! But the real reason for both the messages of Daniel and Yeshua is to alert us to the reality that it is high time to keep our eyes on the existing Temple Mount and do precisely what Yeshua told us to do: "*Watch*" so that we can be on line for what His Father directs us to do next. May I repeat that our opening

---

13.   Dan. 12:11.

text forecasts a no-nonsense evacuation rather than solving Bible puzzles, and I fear that those not in the habit of listening to the Holy Spirit for guidance may be in for somewhat of a problem. Nor do I presume that the message is reserved for Judea alone. Worldwide terrorist attacks are growing in intensity and are knowing fewer and fewer impenetrable national boundaries.

And that brings us back to that soon-to-come violent confrontation over Jerusalem.

The Jewish people, who have yearned and proclaimed, "Next year in Jerusalem," at their Passover Seders for nearly 2,000 years, have once again returned to their cherished city, which is the indisputable heart and soul of every true Jew on the face of the earth. In 1967, both Eastern and Western halves of the city were once again reunited after a 19-year hiatus, the Jordanians, having had seized control over Eastern Jerusalem at the time of the Israeli battle for independence in 1948. Finally, at the lightning climax of the Six-Day War, to the disbelief of the nations of the world at large, the 19-year-old blue and white *Magen David* of Israel, fluttered in triumph over a united Jerusalem back under the sovereignty of her God-appointed tenants.[14] Battle-hardened soldiers alongside their rabbis, who represented the spiritual core of the nation, wept together in thanksgiving to their God at the ruins of the foundation stones of their ancient but nonetheless beloved temple. Jerusalem is mentioned over 800 times in the Scriptures and is perhaps the only real estate on earth that so exemplifies the heartbeat of a nation. No real Jew, no matter how secular or removed from his ancient faith, would ever have the raw nerve to willingly relinquish control of his eternal capital again.

And the owners of the two mosques looked on. Islam has its own sentiments. Though never once mentioned in the Koran, next to Medina and Mecca in Saudi Arabia, Jerusalem is deemed as the third most holy place in the Islamic world. Chairman Arafat threatens almost daily that if he doesn't get Jerusalem as the capital for his proposed "Palestinian State," the resultant violence the Jews can expect will be an eruption out of control.

---

14. Lev. 25:23 NIV.

Where Is the Body?

All the while, 22 Muslim Arab neighbors menacingly look on in a brotherhood of agreement, with only two of the so-called "moderates," Jordan and Egypt, ever having had signed pledges of peace on paper with Israel. The extremists, Iran (Muslims, but not Arabs), Iraq, Syria, and Libya, are preparing—or already have prepared—clandestine non-conventional arsenals of missiles equipped with deadly chemical or biological warheads, with the former two vying for even more devastating nuclear capacity as well. If there is war—or should we say when—Islamic brothers must become brothers. There is an old Arab proverb: "The enemy of my enemy is my friend." One must understand the Arab psyche to comprehend the reasoning.[15] No matter what internal rivalries may exist among the Arabs, any real or imagined issue against the Jews, will cause their blood to join together in blissful harmony. Moreover, the dictator, president, or *ayatollah* who can, for whatever reason, land the ultimate death blow upon despised Israel, will earn not only the highest accolades of prestige among his brethren in this life, but will also expect unbelievable goodies from Allah in the world to come! These are Israel's nearest neighbors.

And with that backdrop, the hinges on the door of destiny—not only for the Middle East but for the entire globe—both now and forever, swing on the city of Jerusalem. Read your Bible!

Who should be surprised? Although we have already looked at part of the following text in Chapter 10, the present context demands that we focus on it once more. Over two and a half millennia ago, the Hebrew prophet Zechariah proclaimed:

> *This is the word of the Lord concerning Israel. The Lord, who stretches out the heavens, who lays the foundation of the earth, and who forms the spirit of man within him, declares: "I am going to make Jerusalem a cup that sends all the surrounding peoples reeling. Judah will be besieged as well as Jerusalem. On that day, when **all the nations** of the earth are gathered*

---

15. Again, we refer the reader to *Philistine* by Ramon Bennett for an in-depth study of the Arab mind and the Islamic world view.

152

against her, I will make Jerusalem an immovable rock for all the nations. All who try to move it will injure themselves" (Zechariah 12:1-3).

Well, there is our rock and there is our hard place! It has been pro-grammed from the database of time, and the Almighty has given us as well a script to follow for the finale. It may be of interest that Jerusalem has been besieged over the ages by the Romans, the Babylonians, the Assyrians, and a spate of other invaders but never by *all the nations*. This one has been reserved for us to watch on TV—that is if you still happen to be in the house. And if CNN still happens to be on air!

A second witness to reinforce Zechariah is recorded by the prophet Joel. Again, we looked at this text in part in Chapter 10, but in our pres-ent discussion on Jerusalem, we must underline it once more:

*In those days and at that time, when I restore the fortunes of Judah and Jerusalem, I will gather **all nations** and bring them down to the Valley of Jehoshaphat. There I will enter into judg-ment against them concerning My inheritance, My people Israel, for they scattered My people among the nations and divided up My land* (Joel 3:1-2).

In case it has slipped your mind just exactly where the Valley of Jehoshaphat is located, we will review that it is *not* another name for Armageddon. The Valley of Armageddon generates similar overtones, but it is a projected hot spot at another place, but quite possibly not for another time. We will have a look at Armageddon shortly.

But Jehoshaphat is another name for the diminutive Kidron Valley that Jesus crossed over as He and the disciples left the upper room enroute to Gethsemane.[16] It's the small seasonally dry *wadi* that separates the Mount of Olives from Jerusalem proper, and little more than 15 min-utes walk from the heart of Old Jerusalem. It is known today as East Jeru-salem, and it is the home of tens of thousands of Palestinians. The media frequently refers to the area as "Arab Jerusalem," which disturbs me to

---

16. Jn. 18:1.

no small measure. Firstly, Israel *does* hold the political sovereignty over the whole of the city, but on an even higher authority than that, I find nothing about an "Arab" Jerusalem in my Bible—nor even in the Koran for that matter. But let's not let the facts get in the way of a lovely twist of anti-Israeli propaganda!

Unfortunately, Kidron—or shall we say Jehoshaphat—is highly infiltrated these days by militants which make it a breeding ground for terrorists. Several homemade bombs for killing Jews were suspected of having come out of the general area, and the scenario for Joel's prophecy is ready-made. The specific location is a tinderbox. Never has there been a time in history when all the precise details of these two complimenting prophecies, have been so close around the corner.

And to those two pronouncements, we join a third, parallel text, once more from Zechariah, which follows quite on the heels of his Jerusalem prophecy above:

> *I will gather **all the nations** to Jerusalem to fight against it; the city will be captured, the houses ransacked, and the women raped. Half of the city will go into exile, but the rest of the people will not be taken from the city. Then the Lord will go out and fight against those nations, as He fights in the day of battle. On that day His feet will stand on the Mount of Olives, east of Jerusalem, and the Mount of Olives will be split in two from east to west, forming a great valley, with half of the mountain moving north and half moving south...then the Lord my God will come and all the holy ones with Him* (Zechariah 14:2-5).

As we detailed in Chapter 10, a further coordinated flow on from these three very precise prophecies, is the intervention of Almighty God through His Messiah at the final battle for Jerusalem. Without noting the Valley of Jehoshaphat by name, the identical advent of Messiah is also catalogued in Matthew Chapter 24, in Paul's communications both to the Corinthian church as well as to the believers in Thessalonica, and finally in the dramatic rescue of the *two olive tree* witnesses in chapter 11 of Revelation.

Prophecies Near and...Far-Out

Now it stands to reason that the Western World is not ordinarily accustomed to seeing the Lord of Hosts just pop out of the sky on any and every occasion. It just doesn't happen, and we tend to subconsciously "know" that it doesn't happen. So we mentally just keep pushing the return of the Messiah back about one or two decades at a time so that we won't have to intellectually deal with it.

Know what? If it's as true as what we *profess* we believe about what our Bibles tell us, it *is* going to happen sooner or later. And with what we see shaping up in Jerusalem at the time of this writing, it appears it will be much sooner rather than a little later!

Yeshua didn't tell us to calculate. He told us to *watch* vigilantly. Thus, it boggles the mind to ascertain what is formulating in the heads of those professed believers who have little interest and even less clues with regard to what is currently going on in "the place where the Lord your God chooses to put His Name."[17] Israel is the fuse to the time bomb, the stop watch for the event and the venue of the return all wrapped up in one.

To be sure, there is little credibility left in the media these days, but that is merely due to their unsavory predisposition to *interpret* the news rather than *present* it. They will, of course, tell you when they perceive that Jerusalem is about to go up in a puff of smoke (read: blaze of glory), except that their presentation will include the following:

1. The whole thing is Israel's fault.
2. It has been perpetrated by intransigent "hard-liner" Jews (read: God-fearing).
3. A "peaceful solution" (read: elimination of the State of Israel) is continually being blocked by Israel.
4. "Right wing" settlers (read: *Tanakh* believers) are the "*greatest obstacle to peace.*"

But if you know your Bible—not to mention your God—you should not have any major problem with a skewed media report. In similar vein,

---

17. Deut. 12:21, along with some 20 similar references throughout Deuteronomy.

there are ample Bible-oriented Christian information services from the Internet to up-to-date newsletters and periodicals—that provide an accurate pulse on the times. The wise will certainly make it a priority.

And finally in that realm of soon-to-be anticipated realities, let's have a brief insight into the oft-clichéd Armageddon. In these days of skepticism, Armageddon has become such a well-worn byword that few there be that have a handle on the actual countdown. To be sure, Armageddon is not the Valley of Jehoshaphat, and the Valley of Jehoshaphat is not Armageddon. Armageddon is a major plain some 90 km. north of Jerusalem as the jet flies and considerably further by road. Because of its geographical accessibility and unobstructed terrain, it has been the route of invaders between Asia Minor and Africa for millennia. And today it still lies at the vital crossroads of Israel's heartland.

In chapters 38 and 39 of Ezekiel, the prophet graphically details a horrific end of days invasion and battle on the "mountains of Israel."[18] Though not specifically mentioned by Ezekiel, it is without question the most descriptive account of the long-since popularized, publicized and even fantasized Armageddon, the final battle of the ages. A shorter parallel reference is covered in the Book of Revelation.[19] Far beyond any statistical probabilities of coincidence, prophet Ezekiel's ancient text ironically lists three of the four major players of that final drama to be Iran, Sudan, and Libya, which just happen to be the most vitriolic and hate-filled enemies that Israel has today. The fourth, the one who actually leads the attack, is cryptically known as "King Gog," but it is otherwise unnamed.[20] And to add to the further incredibility of the 2,500-year-old prophecy, all of the three above mentioned nations have turned a corner to magnify the intensity of their present hatred only within the last three decades!

Without the divine direction from the Ancient of Days, how could any prophet from that dim and distant age even begin to get it half right?

18. Ezek. 38:8.

19. Rev. 16:12-21.

20. Ezek. 38:1-5.

Prophecies Near and...Far-Out

Moreover, many more of the details of the prophet's predictions have an unbelievably authentic ring for the nuclear age in which we live, not to mention the rockets that are currently being rattled by Israel's less than congenial neighbors. Moreover there is a strong consensus of increasingly disillusioned Israelis who are awakening to the reality that the illusory and ill-advised "land for peace" formula pressed upon Israel by the international community will ultimately climax with Israel's seventh war for survival since independence in 1948. Will this be the big one?

It is most realistic that for number seven, the now well-armed Palestinian terrorists will explode from within the country—most specifically in East Jerusalem and environs—while Arab armies will once again attack Israel from without with missiles, tanks, and troops. But this time, at long last, the Palestinian entity is desperately lobbying for support of the entire world community. And the only logical land route for the tanks and the troops that would invade with the sought for international blessing is, of course, the Valley of Armageddon. Thus the Valley of Armageddon-Valley of Jehoshaphat axis of attack is now a very real probability, and will most likely be staged concurrently with the hope of finally crushing an Israel that will be spread far too thin.[21]

We have focused primarily on the struggle for Jerusalem because at the time of this writing this has been the point of escalating confrontation which carries little suggestion of going away. To the contrary, it is mushrooming. Suffice it to say that the current political climate in Israel proper, added to the condemnation against Israel worldwide, lends dramatically to the fast approaching scenario for both battles of Jerusalem and Armageddon to formulate at very short notice. But the contest for Jerusalem, which includes the prophesied venue for our Lord's return, is at these moments of mounting agitation, the most relevant scenario to monitor.

So for your own awareness and preparation, keep your eyes on "the place where the Lord your God [has chosen] to put His Name."[22]

---

21. "War in Israel in 1999?" *Middle East Intelligence Digest*: Internet Edition, July 13, 1998.

22. Deut. 12:21, along with some 20 similar references throughout Deuteronomy.

Where Is the Body?

And finally a command from the Scripture that must be repeated:

I have posted watchmen on your walls, O Jerusalem; they will never be silent day or night. You who call on the Lord, give yourselves no rest, and give Him no rest until He establishes Jerusalem and makes her the praise of the earth (Isaiah 62:6-7).

Chapter 14

Where Is the Body?

In final summary, our most significant concern throughout these pages has been to positively identify our Lord's spiritual body—the *Body* He uniquely left behind as He returned to His Father. Where is it? Who is it? And why?

We have dealt with the concept of His Body at great length particularly in Chapter 5, concluding from text upon text of New Testament Scripture that in the Sovereign God's eternal plan there can be one and one only *Body*, a body being prepared, groomed, and consecrated as the cherished Bride of the Messiah. Is this the Gentile Church as so many purport? Not quite—at least not by itself—if you give any real credence to the entire panorama of Scriptures which that Church professes to believe.

The only credible and complete body of Messiah must be a composite of *Jew* and *Gentile* as conceived, planned and designed by the Father God going all the way back to His eternal promise of the inheritance to Abraham through which, "all peoples on earth will be blessed through you."[1] Unless one frantically cuts and pastes and deliberately discards whole sections of the Holy Writ at will, you will find no other body in the Book than the one that contains Gentile believers conceived and

---

1.   Gen. 12:3.

embedded within the original family of promise—the extended and completed family of Abraham.

Thus, with scriptural authority, we must acknowledge, in our heads at least, that the *Body* is an actual fact made up of Gentile believers grafted into an original Jewish foundation. Semantic understanding, however, gives assent to that which is not always "audio visual." That is, we may never have to touch the reality of what we concede with our supposedly "spiritually clean" hands!

Therefore, to actually grasp a readjusted concept of the Body of our Lord in what we have come to know as the "Church Age" may, on one hand, come as a temporary relief to those among us whose theological boundaries long ago became embedded in concrete to concede that, in the end of it all, the Almighty does retain the right to pull off some surprises.

But on the other hand, this concession is a contradiction in terms, which in itself will cause the Western technical mind no small discomfort. We much prefer our data base to produce predictable results with precision accuracy. Indeed, our limitations of human exactitude make it most difficult to comprehend a God whose dimensions of time are quite unlike our own where His view of the end of days is of little temporal consequence in relation to the beginning of time. By sheer contrast, He sees His composite Body very distinctly, viewing the whole as one precisely defined unit—that which was, what is, and what will be. This not only defines our Lord Himself, but also His visual embrace of His entire universe as well.

Unfortunately, our vision is not quite that good, even though we frequently delude ourselves into thinking that it is. But the better you get to know Him, you come to understand that the God of the Bible includes what He will include, forgives what He will forgive, discards what He will discard, and redeems what He will redeem. He does and will have the last word!

But in this case, His final word will be what He has promised to orchestrate among His Jewish family in days soon to come. If your problem is "not being able to tell the players without a program" (read: church bulletin), and you are uncertain which ones of the remnant may or may not end up in the Kingdom, that's easy. Love them all—and above all, start treating each one like part of the family! You'll be amazed at what your Father and their Father begins to do to close the circle, and that on His terms.

Thus may we be content to let God be God and grace be grace. If you have a problem with this, I suggest you need to reread a good Book on the divine record of God's relationship with His entire extended family—the Bible.

But with all this taken into consideration, just how can we mortals pinpoint the *Body* a bit more precisely at this stage of the Age? Our Lord told His disciples—which includes those of us who believe:

All men will hate you because of Me (Matthew 10:22a)

In a closely related text in Matthew, He more specifically states:

You will be hated by all nations because of Me (Matthew 24:9b)[2]

This declaration further accents our point below.

May we specifically note that our Lord Yeshua did not say "all Jews will hate you" or even "all the religious hierarchy" but "all men." Matthew made it even clearer by stating, "*all nations*," meaning of course, "all Gentiles." Anti-Semitism including subtle, or most often not-so-subtle anti-Jewishness within the Church itself, is a stark fulfillment of this simply stated prophecy. The Gentile believers once also knew this pain of persecution in being torn apart by lions in the arena or bloody beheadings in the dungeons of Rome. But we must again reflect on the axiom we discovered in Chapter 7. *The further the Church moved away from her Hebraic roots, the less the persecution became*! Ponder also that the persecution of a lesser segment of the Gentile Church once again increased from the sixteenth to the nineteenth centuries among the reformist believers in Europe who were seeded with a return to a *biblical orientation*. Attachment to the Scriptures is not only a bedrock Jewish tradition, but the Bible itself is predominantly of Hebrew origin.

Today the Church has been treated with a relatively positive respect in almost all nations, the Muslim-dominated countries being a few of the

---

2.   See also Mk. 13:13; Lk. 21:17.

exceptions. The Jew has not. Where the Church's revised heritage and manipulated theologies have turned a blind eye to her real roots, she has quite purged herself from any uncomfortable Jewish stigma and has become a tolerable entity for the world to live with. The God-fearing Jew never has.

Why? How can a Jew who has never recognized the authenticity of Yeshua as Messiah be hated by all men because of Him? Contrariwise, how can a noble churchman with cross in hand be honored and extolled by a society that has little esteem for eternal values? Perhaps we may be dealing with more than one Jesus—one Jesus reflects His true Father, while the other idolatrously represents the mere figurehead of a system! Consequently, it is not only the Jewish Jesus that is despised, *but the God of Abraham whose image He reflects.*

So whether it be a true Gentile believer in Yeshua as Lord or the no-nonsense, God-fearing Jew who has yet to encounter the real Jewish Jesus—if he is marching to the beat of the wrong drummer, he will generate no joy in a hostile, humanistic system. I challenge you to check it out. Again, Jesus said what He meant and meant what He said. The world system has neither time nor taste for the God that Yeshua represents.

A capsulated summary of the mentality of most materialistically oriented Gentiles is the classic quote:

How odd
Of God
To choose
The Jews.[3]

But a far more biblically oriented response has been:

But not so odd
As those who choose
A Jewish God
But spurn the Jews.[4]

---

3. From the writings of William Norman Ewer, American journalist-poet, 1885-1976 as cited from the personal files of Moshe Kohn, columnist for "View from Nov," *Jerusalem Post*, Jersualem.

4. Lewis Cecil Browne, "How Odd of God" (1934), from the personal files of Moshe Kohn.

Where Is the Body?

Thus, the no-nonsense disciples of Jesus will find a double source of rejection. His teaching of an alternate Kingdom of selflessness in a world whose axis rotates on competition is something less than popular. And then there is our Lord's family members who also tend to be a bit of a problem. Any warm identity with them needs to be kept privately tucked away in the "thought closet" when any and all anti-Semites happen to drift into our conversational circles. It's just not the "in" thing for most of the Christian spectrum to regard Jews as a credible spiritual entity of even some degree for the simple reason that *they are Jews*—the family of Yeshua.

Yet we must understand that we're in this thing together, a Jewish remnant plus Gentile believer alike—whether or not all parts of the *Body* happen to realize it, whether or not all parts of the *Body* happen to personally approve the plan. It's the way the Father of Abraham designed it in the beginning and, like it or not, that's the way it will end up, and that is quite according to the Scriptures!

Yes, Paul, now many of us only "see through a glass, darkly."[5]

But there are a couple more Scripture texts that up to this point may seem to be as fuzzy as the definition of the *total* Body of Christ by many who otherwise regard themselves as Christian.

One day when Jesus was speaking to His disciples about the Kingdom of God they curiously asked Him, "Where, Lord?"

His response,

Where the body is, there too will the vultures gather (Luke 17:37 NJB).[6]

A beautifully cryptic reply! When informally chatting with a gifted colleague in Bible translation, I referred to my utter fascination with this comment of Jesus and his jovial rejoinder was, "There are about 38 interpretations to this verse already, so you might as well go for one more!"

---

5. 1 Cor. 13:12 KJV.

6. See also Mt. 24:28.

Not really. Although I prefer not to formally postulate a presumed number 39 for my readers, if I may merely motivate your thinking, that will do as far as I'm concerned. You can draw your own conclusions.

Does it apply or not? As we finalize this search for the complete and entire *Body* of our Lord, with one eye on the inhospitable vultures, let us focus our attention on two other intriguing scriptural parallels of dead carcasses. May we never lose grip on our "Two or Three Principle" to the very end!

The first instance, we have already covered in depth in Chapters 9 and 10, when we observed that an inhumane beast would hew the *two olive tree* witnesses to the ground:

Their bodies will lie in the street of the great city...for three and a half days... (Revelation 11:8-9).

Were those two bodies actually as clinically dead as the party makers of the allegory presumed? For three and a half days? Were there vultures circling overhead waiting for a final dinner call? Would they not have been a little dismayed when their entrees stood up triumphantly to join their Lord in the air to be ever after attached to Him?

But if we continue to pursue textual parallels and a multi-witness of repeat Scriptures there is one final scenario that dare not be overlooked. All the way back to where it began in Chapter 15 of Genesis, Abraham cut a covenant with the Almighty to forever seal the promises to him and his entire family for all generations. After the Lord instructed Abraham in the exact animal sacrifices He wanted him to offer:

*He brought Him all these, split the animals down the middle and placed **each half opposite the other**; but the birds he did not divide. And whenever birds of prey swooped down on the carcasses, Abram drove them off* (Genesis 15:10-11, NJB).

Note that each sacrifice was cut into *two identical halves* and laid out symmetrically before the Lord. Is there a precise meaning in this? Is there a prophetic parallel with the *two olive tree* witnesses of Revelation 11? It is more than a positive assurance to know that One greater than Abraham is among us to drive off the would be devouring vultures.

164

Where Is the Body?

So, *where is the Body?* When half the world distances itself from you because you have a warm corner in your heart for the Jewish family and the other half disparages you because you're a no-nonsense disciple of their elder Brother—the greatest Jew who ever lived—you'll know you're a part of it!

**For international meeting and ministry schedules
or information on the availability of additional copies of this book:**

South Pacific Island Ministries
P.0. Box 990
Smithfield 4878, Queensland, Australia
Tel/Fax within Australia: 07-4058-0258
Tel/Fax International: 617-4058-0258
e-mail: SpimAust@aol.com
www.link-zone.net/spim.html

Book sales in the U.S.A:

Destiny Image® Publishers, Inc.
P.O. Box 310
Shippensburg, PA 17257-0310
Tel: 1-800-722-6774
Fax: 717-532-8646
Internet: www.destinyimage.com

Book sales in Israel:

The Galilee Experience
P.O. Box 1693
Tiberias 14115 Israel
Tel: 972-6-672-3260
Fax: 972-6-672-3195
e-mail: galexp@kinneret.co.il

Recommended Additional Reading

On the Tragic Record of the Church Toward the Jewish People:

> *Our Hands Are Stained With Blood*
> By Dr. Michael Brown
> 1994
> Destiny Image® Publishers, Inc.
> P.O. Box 310
> Shippensburg, PA 17257-0310
> Tel: 1-800-722-6774
> Fax: 717-532-8646
> Internet: http://www.reapernet.com

On the Global Islamic Threat:

> *Philistine*
> By Ramon Bennett
> 1995
> Arm of Salvation Publishing
> Jerusalem
> Available at: Shekinah Books Ltd.
> P.O. Box 846, Keno, OR 97627, U.S.A.
> Tel: 541-882-9777
> Fax: 541-850-4395
> e-mail: shekinah@kfalls.net

On Authoritative Historical Perspective of the Rebirth of Israel:

> *O Jerusalem!*
> By Collins and Lapierre
> 1972
> Simon & Schuster, Hemel Hempstead, U.K.
> Available at any commercial bookstore.

Additional copies of this book and other book titles from DESTINY IMAGE are available at your local bookstore.

For a bookstore near you, call 1-800-722-6774

Send a request for a catalog to:

Destiny Image ® Publishers, Inc.
P.O. Box 310
Shippensburg, PA 17257-0310

*"Speaking to the Purposes of God for This
Generation and for the Generations to Come"*

**For a complete list of our titles,
visit us at www.destinyimage.com**